THE LAWS OF MOTION
AN ANTHOLOGY OF CURRENT THOUGHT

$22.95

Contemporary Discourse
in the Field of
PHYSICS™

The Laws of Motion

An Anthology of Current Thought

Edited by Linley Erin Hall

The Rosen Publishing Group, Inc., New York

Published in 2006 by The Rosen Publishing Group, Inc.
29 East 21st Street, New York, NY 10010

Library of Congress Cataloging-in-Publication Data

The laws of motion: an anthology of current thought/edited by
Linley Erin Hall.—1st ed.
    p. cm.—(Contemporary discourse in the field of physics)
Includes bibliographical references and index.
ISBN 1-4042-0408-3 (lib. bdg.)
1. Motion—History. 2. Dynamics—History. 3. Mechanics—
History. 4. Scattering (Physics) I. Hall, Linley Erin. II. Series.
QC133.L39 2006
531—dc22

                                                    2005000925

Manufactured in the United States of America

On the cover (clockwise from top right): Patterns of light on a
white surface; the motion of a ball's parabolic bounce captured
under a strobe light; portrait of Sir Isaac Newton; liquid crystal.

CONTENTS

Introduction

Motion surrounds us in ways that other observable physical phenomena do not. Every time you walk, throw a ball, lean forward to whisper in a friend's ear, dance, stand up, sit down, or stretch, you are in motion. Things around you are in motion as well—cars, raindrops, cats, footballs, Earth's tectonic plates. Even the air around you moves.

Scientists, philosophers, and the curious had tested the laws of motion for thousands of years before Isaac Newton codified them in his work on classical dynamics. Newton also performed research in mathematics, optics, and other fields, and these other explorations informed his work on motion. Certainly, his development of calculus provided a useful tool for solving problems in mechanics.

In 1687, Newton published what is widely regarded as his masterwork, the *Philosophiae Naturalis Principia Mathematica*, more commonly known as the *Principia*. It analyzed the motion of objects under the influence of gravity. The first book set forth what are now known as Newton's three laws of motion, namely:

1. An object at rest stays at rest as long as no net force acts on it.

2. Force is equal to mass times acceleration, or $F = ma$.

3. For every force acting on an object, there is an equal and opposite reaction force acting on another object.

The second book of the *Principia* discussed motion in resisting media, namely fluids. The third book applied the laws of the first book to the solar system. For instance, Newton showed that Johannes Kepler's laws of planetary motion were special cases of universal laws and explained the orbits of comets. The three laws outlined in the first book of the *Principia* give rise to many other concepts and equations. They are so basic to motion that many people refer to Newtonian mechanics or Newtonian dynamics when discussing the movement of familiar objects.

Newtonian dynamics describe quite well the macroscopic objects we encounter often, such as baseballs, tires, and clock pendulums. But the molecules—and atoms and subatomic particles—that make up those everyday, macroscopic objects do not always follow those laws. Rather than having a continuous range of energies, atomic and subatomic particles can only possess discrete, disjointed amounts of energy. In other words, they are quantized. Since energy is essential to motion, quantization has a significant effect on how far, how fast, and in what directions these particles can travel, as well as the consequences when they collide. In quantum mechanics, particles can also travel over and/or through barriers that would be impregnable in classical dynamics.

Since the early 1900s, research in the field of quantum mechanics has produced a large body of theories, equations, and experimental evidence to explain and predict the behavior of quantized particles. With assumptions and idealized conditions, some of these equations can be simplified to the familiar, classical equations of motion. The allowed energies of macroscopic objects are also quantized, but the energy levels are so close together that approximation by the continuous functions of classical dynamics is valid.

Most physicists do not work in the field of motion as such. Newton's laws are so well established and, through experimentation, have been shown to be true so many times that they are no longer very interesting to work on directly. However, researchers do use the basic principles of motion to solve problems in other areas of physics, including astronomy, fluid dynamics, and biophysics. Many scientists are also working to reconcile Newtonian physics with quantum mechanics, which is an important issue facing the physics community.

This anthology presents some of the most current and important research in the field of physics that has expanded our understanding of motion or applied classical dynamics to new and different situations. Many of the articles in this volume look at how researchers are applying the laws of motion to the study of the movements of actual objects in the "real" world, such as soccer balls, insects, and sand. Several articles look at different types of collisions, both elastic and inelastic, and the resulting transfer of momentum. This volume also examines the differences between classical and quantum mechanics and how reconciliation between them may be possible.

The problems that physics students solve can feel idealized, abstract, purely theoretical, and disconnected from the real world. This volume shows the laws of motion at work in real situations that are active areas of research. The equations become more difficult to solve, and the results may not be as elegant, but the underlying physics is rooted in classical dynamics. —*LEH*

The Laws of
Motion Revisited

1

The Leaning Tower of Pisa is supposedly the site of one of the most famous physics experiments of all time. But did Galileo actually drop cannonballs of different masses off the tower and determine that they hit the ground at the same time? Although the story is probably untrue—Galileo did most of his experiments on gravity with inclined planes—humanity has been fascinated with such demonstrations since then, as Robert P. Crease, a philosophy professor at the State University of New York at Stony Brook and a historian at the Brookhaven National Laboratory, explains in this article.

The experiment is simple: drop two dissimilar objects from a height. Everyday observation suggests that heavier objects should fall faster than lighter ones; air resistance can cause this. But in a vacuum, any two objects will fall at the same rate of acceleration—that determined by gravity alone.

In a 2002 poll in Physics World magazine, Galileo's falling body experiment was named *the second most beautiful, just behind the double-slit experiment with electrons, which demonstrates fundamental quantum mechanical principles. —LEH*

"The Legend of the Leaning Tower"
by Robert P. Crease
Physics World, February 2003

Commander David R Scott (2 August 1971, lunar surface): "Well, in my left hand I have a feather; in my right hand, a hammer. And I guess one of the reasons we got here today was because of a gentleman named Galileo, a long time ago, who made a rather significant discovery about falling objects in gravity fields. And we thought: 'Where would be a better place to confirm his findings than on the Moon?'"

[Camera zooms in on Scott's hands. One is holding a feather, the other a hammer. The camera pulls back to show the Falcon—the Apollo 15 landing craft—and the lunar horizon.]

Scott: "And so we thought we'd try it here for you. The feather happens to be, appropriately, a falcon feather for our Falcon. And I'll drop the two of them here and, hopefully, they'll hit the ground at the same time." [Scott releases hammer and feather. They hit the ground at about the same time.]

Scott: "How about that! Mr. Galileo was correct in his findings."

How the Legend Started

The finding mentioned by Commander Scott, namely that objects of different mass fall at the same rate in a vacuum, is associated with a single person (Galileo) and a single place—the Leaning Tower of Pisa. The culprit is Vincenzio Viviani, Galileo's secretary in the final years of his life.

We owe many of the Galilean legends to Viviani's warm biography of the Italian scholar. One is the story of how Galileo climbed the Leaning Tower of Pisa and—"in the presence of other teachers and philosophers and all the students"—showed through repeated experiments that "the velocity of moving bodies of the same composition, but of different weights, moving through the same medium, do not attain the proportion of their weight as Aristotle decreed, but move with the same velocity."

In his own books, Galileo uses thought experiments to argue that objects of unequal mass fall together in a vacuum. Without mentioning the Leaning Tower, he reports having "made the test" with a cannonball and a musket ball. What is perhaps surprising, however, is that Galileo found that the two balls did not quite fall together. This finding—coupled with the fact that Viviani's biography is the only source to mention that the experiments were done at the Leaning Tower—causes most historians of science to doubt Viviani's version of what Galileo did. They believe that the elderly and then-blind Galileo may have misremembered when speaking to his youthful assistant.

Dropping the Ball

Science historians find Galileo's early experiments with falling bodies fascinating, for several reasons. One is that Galileo was not the first. As far back as the sixth century, other scholars who doubted Aristotle's account of motion had also experimented with falling bodies and concluded that Aristotle was wrong. They included several 16th-century Italians and one of Galileo's predecessors as professor at Pisa.

Also intriguing is Galileo's report, based on experiment, that balls of unequal weight do not only fall at different rates, but that the lighter one initially pulls ahead of the heavier one until the heavier catches up. In the early 1980s the science historian Thomas Settle tried to repeat Galileo's falling-body experiments and, astonishingly, noted the same thing. He suggested that fatigue induced in the hand holding the heavier object tends to cause this hand to let go more slowly, even when the dropper believes the objects are released simultaneously.

Yet another fascinating side to Galileo's experiments is the way that they slowly transformed from genuine scientific inquiries into public displays. After Galileo's death, scientists including Robert Boyle and Willem Gravesande built air pumps and special chambers to explore vertical fall in evacuated environments. King George III, for instance, once witnessed a demonstration involving a feather and a one-guinea coin falling together inside an evacuated tube. The popularity of such demonstrations continues to this day, featuring in

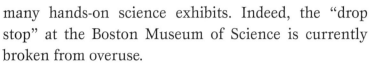

many hands-on science exhibits. Indeed, the "drop stop" at the Boston Museum of Science is currently broken from overuse.

Teachers, no doubt, would call the Apollo "feather-drop" a sloppy experiment. Nobody bothered to measure the height from which the objects were released (probably 110–160 cm). Nobody cared that Scott was leaning over with his arms not parallel to the ground. Nobody measured the time of the fall (on the video it is just above 1 s). But as a demonstration it is unforgettable. The TV coverage—plus the fact that it has a webpage with video clip—makes it possibly the most watched science demonstration ever.

The Critical Point

So why do falling-body experiments continue to be so popular? They were, for example, voted into the top 10 "most beautiful experiments" of all time in my recent poll of *Physics World* readers (September 2002 pp. 19–20). I think the answer is related to the fact that, as everyday experience suggests, heavier bodies do fall faster than light ones. Hammers and golf balls, for example, fall faster than feathers and ping-pong balls. Aristotle had codified this observation into an entire framework that was oriented by the everyday observations he was seeking to explain, involving an agent that exerted a force against resistance. Although this framework fails to incorporate acceleration, it is still the one that we mainly live in and that mainly works for us.

Thus we can still find it enlightening, or even surprising, to see with our very own eyes the expectations of that framework being violated. Galileo played a seminal role in transforming that framework, in developing the abstract thinking involved in the new one, and in illustrating its importance. So what if there was no original experiment? Galileo inspired an entire genre of experiments and demonstrations that allow us to change how we think and see. We might as well refer to these as the offspring of Galileo's experiment at the Leaning Tower of Pisa.

Reprinted with permission from *Physics World*.

Physics students often learn about motion, particularly momentum, by considering balls bouncing off other balls, floors, walls—just about anything, really. The laws of momentum state that it must be conserved, which, among other things, means that a ball dropped vertically onto the floor should bounce straight back up rather than bouncing off at an angle. Momentum is equal to mass times velocity, and vertical velocity cannot become horizontal velocity. However, real materials do not always work as straightforwardly as these idealized balls and walls. This article discusses new research on a case in which an object, such as a ball or disk, hits a softer surface at an angle (rather than perpendicularly) and rebounds with more vertical velocity than it started with. Are

the laws of physics being broken? Researchers have puzzled over this finding for several years, but a new computer model created by Hiroto Kuninaka and Hisao Hayakawa suggests that the mismatch in the hardness of the materials can explain the extra vertical velocity. —LEH

"Getting an Extra Bounce"
by Chelsea Wald
Physical Review Focus, October 4, 2004

Like a gymnast who runs toward a vaulting horse and then hurls herself skyward, a ball can, under certain conditions, rebound from a glancing impact with a surprisingly vertical trajectory. It's a phenomenon that's been observed but never fully explained—and at times even doubted. But now researchers report in the 8 October *PRL* that they have developed a theory that explains the phenomenon and have tested it with computer simulations. Their explanation—which hinges on the ball's impact deforming the surface it hits—could help refine models of the flow of granular materials such as sand dunes, cement, and soil.

The coefficient of normal restitution compares the vertical component of the velocity of an object before and after it has bounced. Conventional wisdom says it's less than one—that is, a ball can't leave the ground moving faster than when it arrived, because that would require extra energy (in the case of the gymnast, her body creates energy). But since the early 1990s several research groups have reported experiments with oblique impacts in which they found what seemed to be absurd results: A hockey-puck-like disk glanced against a wall and then appeared to pop away with an increased perpendicular velocity,[1] and a ceramic sphere rebounded off a softer surface with a noticeably more vertical trajectory.[2]

"They first thought I was crazy!" says Michel Louge of Cornell University, who performed the sphere-bouncing experiment with student Michael Adams. But after carefully ruling out experimental error, he concluded that the ball must deform the surface in such a way that it changes the trajectory of the ball. In that way, he thought, some of the horizontal component of the velocity could be transferred to the vertical component. He wasn't sure exactly how this would happen, although it was clear that the effect was limited to special situations. "My conjecture in the [experimental] paper was just that—a conjecture," he says.

Now Hiroto Kuninaka and Hisao Hayakawa of Kyoto University in Japan report that they have simulated the small-scale interactions between a disk and an elastic surface that can lead to a greater-than-one coefficient of normal restitution. Their computer simulation calculates a coefficient of 1.3 when the disk strikes the surface at an angle of about 11 degrees; at that angle, their simulated ball rebounds at about 15 degrees. The simulation results resemble Louge's experimental data, according to the authors.

The simulation allowed the team to see the virtual disk denting the surface when it hit at oblique angles. Bill Stronge of Cambridge University in England describes the indentation as a kind of ski jump, which redirects the sphere's velocity skyward. Because of this phenomenon, the coefficient of normal restitution can be greater than one without breaking the laws of physics. "The point is that the target material is softer than the ball," says Kuninaka.

But Stronge doubts that the impact could make as vertical a ski jump as the researchers' model suggests. It may have some effect, he says, "but I think that it's certainly not nearly as dramatic as they have portrayed." Computer models of granular materials such as cement and soil must account accurately for the collisions between grains, which can be treated like collisions with walls. So the work could contribute to practical advances in industries that manage and transport these materials, says Louge—and add to the understanding of the physics of ball sports.

References:

[1] J. Calsamiglia, S. W. Kennedy, A. Chatterjee, A. Ruina, and J. T. Jenkins, "Anomalous Frictional Behavior in Collisions of Thin Disks," *J. Appl. Mech.* 66, 146 (1999).

[2] Michel Y. Louge and Michael E. Adams, "Anomalous behavior of normal kinematic restitution in the oblique impacts of a hard sphere on an elastoplastic plate," *Phys. Rev. E* 65, 021303 (2002).

When students are first introduced to physics, the problems often assume that friction is not important. Air resistance is negligible, balls roll

across perfectly smooth surfaces, and so on. In the real world, however, friction is essential for many activities most people take for granted, including simply getting out of bed in the morning. Experimenters must take friction into account if they are to obtain realistic answers.

However, physicists do not really understand how friction works. Several different theories have been proposed, including that dirt is an important factor. This article examines research by Eric Gerde and M. Marder that suggests a new theory of friction based on self-healing cracks. As these cracks separate an object at their leading edge, the object reseals itself at the trailing edge. Experimental evidence supporting this theory is still needed, but it offers an interesting glimpse into a ubiquitous feature of motion in the nonideal world. —LEH

"Surface Physics: A New Crack at Friction"
by David A. Kessler
Nature, September 20, 2001

Friction is a ubiquitous feature of everyday life. Without it, we couldn't walk, tyres wouldn't roll, and ballpoint pens would fail to write. But what is friction, and how does it act?

The basic properties are simple to grasp. To move a solid object from rest on top of a solid surface, a minimum force has to be applied to overcome the force of friction. This force is proportional to the compressive force pushing the two surfaces together, in this case the weight of the object. Intriguingly, this minimum force is independent of the area of contact between the body and the surface. So the friction force on a rectangular solid resting on a table is the same whichever face is in contact with the surface. These laws have been known since the mid 1700s and are attributed to the French physicists Guillaume Amontons (1663–1705) and Charles Augustin de Coulomb (1736–1806). It is one of the dirty little secrets of physics that while we physicists can tell you a lot about quarks, quasars and other exotica, there is still no universally accepted explanation of the basic laws of friction. On page 285 of this issue, Gerde and Marder[1] offer a theory of surface cracks that may lead to a better understanding of surface friction.

The standard picture of friction[2] (dating from as recently as the 1960s) is that the solid surfaces are not really planar, but are rough on a microscopic scale. The presence of these tiny surface features, or asperities as they are known, prevents the surfaces from coming into full contact. So the true contact area is much smaller than its apparent value, and is proportional to the compressive force between the surfaces, in much the same way that the contact area between a car tyre and the road increases when you load your car. Problems have arisen when physicists tried to confirm this picture using calculation from first principles. The goal is to construct, either analytically or on the computer, a solid body and surface from atoms with prescribed interactions, and calculate the friction force directly. But previous attempts at this found that the two surfaces

ride freely on top of each other because of the mismatch between the asperities on the two surfaces, so there is no friction.

Two alternative solutions to the problem have recently been proposed. The first, suggested by Müser, Wenning and Robbins,[3] attributes a crucial role to dirt—the diffuse collection of foreign mobile atoms trapped between the two surfaces. According to the authors' numerical simulations, these mobile atoms quickly find appropriate gaps between the surfaces where they become trapped. These atoms then "lock" the two surfaces in place. To move the top surface, it has to be pushed up and over the dirt atoms, the force required being proportional to the weight of the top body. Furthermore, the calculated force is seen to be essentially independent of the apparent contact area.

Gerde and Marder[1] suggest a second, radically different mechanism, based on the physics of self-healing shear fracture. The basic idea is simple. Imagine you want to move a large rug some distance along the floor. Instead of dragging it, a less back-breaking method is to lift the back edge, slide the edge forward a bit and so introduce a ridge in the rug. Pushing on the ridge moves it forwards along the length of the rug until it reaches the end. The net result is that the rug has been shifted. If one pushed uniformly on the rug and not just on the ridge (a uniform shear load), the ridge would move on its own. In essence, this is a kind of surface fracture; the two surfaces at the ridge (the rug and the floor) are now no longer in contact, just as the two halves of a material break contact and come apart at a crack.

This sort of surface fracture is different to the type created when two surfaces are pulled apart (called a mode I crack). In this case, the surfaces are kept far apart, whereas in the fracture considered by Gerde and Marder (a mode II crack) the two surfaces remain in close proximity and can come together again and bond, or "re-heal," in their new laterally shifted positions. This rebonding sets in some distance downstream of the crack edge, so the crack is of finite length. Such self-healing cracks have been suggested to play a crucial role in the dynamics of earthquakes, and apply wherever two surfaces are sheared relative to one another. The existence of such cracks could help to explain the low amount of heat generated by some earthquakes.

The classic theory of self-healing cracks has been plagued by problems. In the standard mathematical treatment, the two surfaces are predicted to oscillate an infinite number of times, with decreasing wavelength as one approaches the edge of the crack. The meaning of this mathematical nightmare has been unclear, and is the subject of considerable controversy. The situation is reminiscent, though in some sense worse, than the situation for mode I cracks.

In the mode I case, where the surfaces are pulled apart, the classic theory predicts infinite stress at the edge of the crack. This problem was resolved by the work of Leonid Slepyan,[4,5] who used an atomic lattice model to study fractures. Using Slepyan's analytical solution of the problem, it can be shown[6] that in the atomic lattice model the stresses increase in accord with the standard theory as the crack edge is approached, until just a few lattice spacings from the edge. At this point, the true stress saturates, deviating from the predictions of the standard theory. Furthermore, the atomic-lattice calculation predicts the velocity of a propagating crack as a function of the applied stress—a factor that has to be taken from experiments in the standard treatment. Slepyan's theory accomplishes for mode I cracks exactly what we want from a theory of friction: it tells us how to get from the microscopic force laws to a macroscopically measurable quantity, here the crack velocity.

In a mathematical tour de force, Gerde and Marder[1] have succeeded in extending the Slepyan model to a mode II crack of finite length. Here, too, the atomic-lattice solution succeeds where the standard theory fails (at the crack edge). Their model also predicts the minimum shear force required to initiate a propagating crack. Gerde and Marder find that this minimum shear force is roughly proportional to the compressive force pushing the surfaces together. In other words, for the surfaces to move relative to one another, the applied force has to be proportional to the compressive force, as in the Amontons–Coulomb law. The idea then is that, once this minimum force is applied, self-healing cracks are created, causing the surfaces to slide past one another. Gerde and Marder's work is a significant step forward in the theory of cracks. Whether it also helps to solve the problem of friction, or whether some other theory along the lines of that put forward by Müser, Wenning and Robbins[3] will prove more fruitful, remains to be seen. It can be hoped that these studies will stimulate new experiments to decide the issue.

References

1. Gerde, E. & Marder, M. *Nature* 413, 285–288 (2001).
2. Bowden, F. P. & Tabor, D. *The Friction and Lubrication of Solids* (Clarendon, Oxford, 1986).
3. Müser, M. H., Wenning, L. & Robbins, M. O. *Phys. Rev. Lett.* 86, 1295–1298 (2001).
4. Slepyan, L. I. *Izv. Akad. Nauk SSSR Mekh. Tverd.* Tela 16, 101–115 (1982).
5. Kulamekhtova, Sh. A., Saraikin, V. A. & Slepyan, L. I. *Izv. Akad. Nauk SSSR Mekh. Tverd.* Tela 19, 112–118 (1984).
6. Kessler, D. A. & Levine, H. *Phys. Rev. E* 59, 5154–5164 (1999).

2 The Laws of Motion in Everyday Life

Many people notice the laws of motion most often while watching and playing sports. A pass down the American football field exhibits projectile motion. A tennis racket transfers momentum to the tennis ball, sending it zooming in the other direction. Friction slows down the baseball player sliding into third. In European football, called soccer in America, players often kick the ball in such a way that it curves into the goal. The 2002 film Bend It Like Beckham introduced this phenomenon to many non-soccer enthusiasts. But what are the physics behind the curved kick?

This article by Takeshi Asai and Takao Akatsuka explains that a specific combination of speed and spin on the ball is needed to achieve a scoring bend. The article also discusses research on how players, both professional and amateur, actually kick the ball—and how that affects the ball's motion. Similar research is being conducted in a variety of different sports to discover improvements to shoes, balls, and other equipment that will maximize performance.

This research may be driven by economics—Americans spent more than $45 million on sporting goods in 2003—but it also provides new insights into motion. —LEH

"The Physics of Football"
by Takeshi Asai and Takao Akatsuka
PhysicsWeb, June 1998

Bill Shankly, the former manager of Liverpool football club, once said: "Football is not about life or death. It is more important than that." This month at the World Cup in France, millions of football fans will get that same feeling for a few, short weeks. Then the event will be over, and all that will remain will be a few repeats on television and the endless speculation about what might have happened. It is this aspect of football that its fans love, and others hate. What if that penalty had gone in? What if the player hadn't been sent off? What if that free kick hadn't bent around the wall and gone in for a goal?

Many fans will remember the free kick taken by the Brazilian Roberto Carlos in a tournament in France last summer. The ball was placed about 30 m from his opponents' goal and slightly to the right. Carlos hit the ball so far to the right that it initially cleared the wall of defenders by at least a metre and made a ball-boy, who stood metres from the goal, duck his head. Then, almost magically, the ball curved to the left and entered the top right-hand corner of the goal—to the amazement of players, the goalkeeper and the media alike.

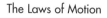

Apparently, Carlos practised this kick all the time on the training ground. He intuitively knew how to curve the ball by hitting it at a particular velocity and with a particular spin. He probably did not, however, know the physics behind it all.

Aerodynamics of Sports Balls

The first explanation of the lateral deflection of a spinning object was credited by Lord Rayleigh to work done by the German physicist Gustav Magnus in 1852. Magnus had actually been trying to determine why spinning shells and bullets deflect to one side, but his explanation applies equally well to balls. Indeed, the fundamental mechanism of a curving ball in football is almost the same as in other sports such as baseball, golf, cricket and tennis.

Consider a ball that is spinning about an axis perpendicular to the flow of air across it. The air travels faster relative to the centre of the ball where the periphery of the ball is moving in the same direction as the airflow. This reduces the pressure, according to Bernouilli's principle. The opposite effect happens on the other side of the ball, where the air travels slower relative to the centre of the ball. There is therefore an imbalance in the forces and the ball deflects—or, as Sir J J Thomson put it in 1910, "the ball follows its nose." This lateral deflection of a ball in flight is generally known as the "Magnus effect."

The forces on a spinning ball that is flying through the air are generally divided into two types: a lift force and a drag force. The lift force is the upwards or sidewards force that is responsible for the Magnus effect. The drag force acts in the opposite direction to the path of the ball.

Let us calculate the forces at work in a well taken free kick. Assuming that the velocity of the ball is 25–30 ms^{-1} (about 70 mph) and that the spin is about 8–10 revolutions per second, then the lift force turns out to be about 3.5 N. The regulations state that a professional football must have a mass of 410–450 g, which means that it accelerates by about 8 ms^{-2}. And since the ball would be in flight for 1 s over its 30 m trajectory, the lift force could make the ball deviate by as much as 4 m from its normal straight-line course. Enough to trouble any goalkeeper!

The drag force, F_D, on a ball increases with the square of the velocity, v, assuming that the density, ρ, of the ball and its cross-sectional area, A, remain unchanged: $F_D = C_D \rho A v^2 / 2$. It appears, however, that the "drag coefficient," C_D, also depends on the velocity of the ball. For example, if we plot the drag coefficient against Reynold's number—a non-dimensional parameter equal to $\rho v D / \mu$, where D is the diameter of the ball and μ is the kinematic viscosity of the air—we find that the drag coefficient drops suddenly when the airflow at the surface of the ball changes from being smooth and laminar to being turbulent.

When the airflow is laminar and the drag coefficient is high, the boundary layer of air on the surface of the ball "separates" relatively early as it flows over the ball, producing vortices in its wake. However, when the airflow is turbulent, the boundary layer sticks to the ball for longer. This produces late separation and a small drag.

The Reynold's number at which the drag coefficient drops therefore depends on the surface roughness of the ball. For example, golf balls, which are heavily dimpled, have quite a high surface roughness and the drag coefficient drops at a relatively low Reynold's number ($\sim 2 \times 10^4$). A football, however, is smoother than a golf ball and the critical transition is reached at a much higher Reynold's number ($\sim 4 \times 10^5$).

The upshot of all of this is that a slow-moving football experiences a relatively high retarding force. But if you can hit the ball fast enough so that the airflow over it is turbulent, the ball experiences a small retarding force. A fast-moving football is therefore double trouble for a goalkeeper hoping to make a save—not only is the ball moving at high speed, it also does not slow down as much as might be expected. Perhaps the best goalkeepers intuitively understand more physics than they realize.

In 1976 Peter Bearman and colleagues from Imperial College, London, carried out a classic series of experiments on golf balls. They found that increasing the spin on a ball produced a higher lift coefficient and hence a bigger Magnus force. However, increasing the velocity at a given spin reduced the lift coefficient. What this means for a football is that a slow-moving ball with a lot of spin will have a larger sideways force than a fast-moving ball with the same spin. So as a ball slows down at the end of its trajectory, the curve becomes more pronounced.

Roberto Carlos Revisited

How does all of this explain the free kick taken by Roberto Carlos? Although we cannot be entirely sure, the following is probably a fair explanation of what went on.

Carlos kicked the ball with the outside of his left foot to make it spin anticlockwise as he looked down onto it. Conditions were dry, so the amount of spin he gave the ball was high, perhaps over 10 revolutions per second. Kicking it with the outside of his foot allowed him to hit the ball hard, at probably over 30 ms^{-1} (70 mph). The flow of air over the surface of the ball was turbulent, which gave the ball a relatively low amount of drag. Some way into its path—perhaps around the 10 m mark (or at about the position of the wall of defenders)—the ball's velocity dropped such that it entered the laminar flow regime. This substantially increased the drag on the ball, which made it slow down even more. This enabled the sideways Magnus force, which was bending the ball towards the goal, to come even more into effect. Assuming that the amount of spin had not decayed too much, then the drag coefficient increased. This introduced an even larger sideways force and caused the ball to bend further. Finally, as the ball slowed, the bend became more exaggerated still (possibly due to the increase in the lift coefficient) until it hit the back of the net—much to the delight of the physicists in the crowd.

Current Research into Football Motion

There is more to football research than simply studying the motion of the ball in flight. Researchers are also interested in finding out how a footballer actually kicks a ball. For example, Stanley Plagenhof of the University of Massachusetts in the US has studied the kinematics of kicking—in other words, ignoring the forces involved. Other researchers, such as Elizabeth Roberts and co-workers at the University of Wisconsin, have done dynamic analyses of kicking, taking the forces involved into account.

These experimental approaches have produced some excellent results, although many challenges still remain. One of the most critical problems is the difficulty of measuring the physical motion of humans, partly because their movements are so unpredictable. However, recent advances in analysing motion with computers have attracted much attention in sports science, and, with the help of new scientific methods, it is now possible to make reasonably accurate measurements of human motion.

For example, two of the authors (TA and TA) and a research team at Yamagata University in Japan have used a computational scientific approach coupled with the more conventional dynamical methods to simulate the way players kick a ball. These simulations have enabled the creation of "virtual" soccer players of various types—from beginners and young children to professionals—to play in virtual space and time on the computer. Sports equipment manufacturers, such as the ASICS Corporation, who are sponsoring the Yamagata project, are also interested in the work. They hope to use the results to design safer and higher performance sports equipment that can be made faster and more economically than existing products.

The movement of players was followed using high-speed video at 4500 frames per second, and the impact of the foot on the ball was then studied with finite-element analysis. The initial experiments proved what most footballers know: if you strike the ball straight on with your instep so that the foot hits the ball in line with the ball's centre of gravity, then the ball shoots off in a straight line. However, if you kick the ball with the front of your foot and with the angle between your leg and foot at 90°, it will curve in flight. In this case, the impact is off-centre. This causes the applied force to act as a torque, which therefore gives the ball a spin.

The experimental results also showed that the spin picked up by the ball is closely related to the coefficient of friction between the foot and the ball, and to the offset distance of the foot from the ball's centre of gravity. A finite-element model of the impact of the foot on the ball, written with DYTRAN and PATRAN software from the MacNeal Schwendler Corporation, was used to numerically analyse these events. This study showed that an increase in the coefficient of friction between the ball and the foot caused the ball to acquire more spin. There was also more spin if the offset position was further from the centre of gravity. Two other interesting effects were observed. First, if the offset distance increased, then the foot touched the ball for a shorter time and over a smaller area, which caused both the spin and the velocity of the ball to decrease. There is therefore an optimum place to hit the ball if you want maximum spin: if you hit the ball too close or too far from the centre of gravity, it will not acquire any spin at all.

The other interesting effect was that even if the coefficient of friction is zero, the ball still gains some spin if you kick it with an offset from its centre of gravity. Although in this case there is no peripheral force parallel to the circumference of the ball (since the coefficient of friction is zero), the ball nevertheless deforms towards its centre, which causes some force to act around the centre of gravity. It is therefore possible to spin a football on a rainy day, although the spin will be much less than if conditions were dry.

Of course, the analysis has several limitations. The air outside the ball was ignored, and it was assumed that the air inside the ball behaved according to a compressive, viscous fluid-flow model. Ideally, the air both inside and outside the ball should be included, and the viscosities modelled using Navier-Stokes equations. It was also assumed that the foot was homogeneous, when it is obvious that a real foot is much more complicated than this. Although it would be impossible to create a perfect model that took every factor into account, this model does include the most important features.

Looking to the future, two of us (TA and TA) also plan to investigate the effect of different types of footwear on the kicking of a ball. Meanwhile, ASICS is combining the Yamagata finite-element simulations with biomechanics, physiology and materials science to design new types of football boots. Ultimately, however, it is the footballer who makes the difference—and without ability, technology is worthless.

The Final Whistle

So what can we learn from Roberto Carlos? If you kick the ball hard enough for the airflow over the surface to become turbulent, then the drag force remains small and the ball will *really* fly. If you want the ball to curve, give it lots of spin by hitting it off-centre. This is easier on a dry day than on a wet day, but can still be done regardless of conditions. The ball will curve most when it slows down into the laminar flow regime, so you need to practise to make sure that this transition occurs in the right place—for example, just after the ball has passed a defensive wall. If conditions are wet, you can still get spin, but you would be better off drying the ball (and your boots).

Nearly 90 years ago J. J. Thomson gave a lecture at the Royal Institution in London on the dynamics of golf balls. He is quoted as saying the following: "If we could accept the explanations of the behaviour of the ball given by many contributors to the very voluminous literature which has collected around the game . . . I should have to bring before you this evening a new dynamics, and announce that matter, when made up into [golf] balls obeys laws of an entirely different character from those governing its action when in any other conditions." In football, at least, we can be sure that things have moved on.

Reprinted with permission from *Physics World*.

One of the most startling discoveries to emerge from the study of quantum mechanics is the ability of particles to move from one location to another through a barrier that was thought to be impassable. This phenomenon, known as quantum or dynamical tunneling, often manifests itself as a particle suddenly being someplace it should not be able to reach or traveling in a different direction than it should be. Researchers had observed dynamical tunneling on the atomic level, but the experiments discussed in this article, which used ultracold particles made of millions of atoms, are two of only a handful to show that the phenomenon is possible for larger systems. The collections of ultracold atoms used in this work are not quite macroscopic. It is unlikely that we will be able to observe dynamical tunneling of baseballs or birds anytime soon, for example. However, every new piece of evidence helps bring classical and quantum physics more in line with one another. —LEH

"Quantum Physics: Air Juggling and Other Tricks"
by Eric J. Heller
Nature, July 5, 2001

An old joke goes like this: a motorist stops to ask a farmer how to get to a village a few miles away. After much thought, the farmer says with conviction: "You can't get there from here."

The farmer may have been a classical physicist. Given constraints such as energy conservation, certain types of motion are isolated in classical systems—one type never leads to the other. Usually we think of a hill or energy barrier preventing the journey, but often the barriers are more subtle and indirect. Imagine a ball bouncing between two semicircular mirrors. Classical dynamics forever confines it to the region between the mirrors, even though there is no energy barrier preventing it leaving through one of the open gaps. Classical motion does not allow escape, but quantum mechanics is famous for allowing tunnelling into classically forbidden barriers, and even right through them.

Can quantum systems wriggle out of subtler, dynamical barriers like those presented by the two mirrors? Absolutely. Delicate experiments in the Phillips laboratory[1] (described on page 52 of this issue), and in the Raizen laboratory[2] (published by *Science*), demonstrate "dynamical tunnelling"[3-5] of ultracold atoms, which allows them to transfer between two stable, but classically separate, states of motion.

Dynamical tunnelling is a close cousin of "above-barrier reflection," in which a particle with enough energy to go over a barrier is nonetheless reflected back—an event forbidden by classical physics. This is also sometimes called diffraction, but this term is used in so many contexts (some of them classically forbidden, some not) that it is best avoided. Dynamical tunnelling can have remarkable and non-intuitive consequences. Consider the formaldehyde molecule, H_2CO, spinning about the C–O axis with the oxygen atom pointing up.

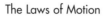

Classically, the oxygen is doomed to point up forever, but in quantum mechanics it can oscillate between pointing up and down. It does this without violating the conservation of energy or angular momentum. In reality, a rotating formaldehyde molecule that starts with oxygen pointing up does flip its direction, just as predicted by quantum mechanics.

By using relatively large numbers of atoms, the Phillips and Raizen groups[1, 2] have caught extremely cold quantum gases in the act of doing something impossible for classical particles. The atoms were put into a very distinct kind of motion, but were later seen in the wrong place at the wrong time (if they had continued to behave classically). Specifically, they were caught travelling in the wrong direction—a feat that is possible only if they had used dynamical tunnelling to get there. Classical particles would need a specific kick to change their direction.

The two groups of experimentalists used a web of crossed laser beams to create elaborate three-dimensional force fields in which the intensity of the light varies periodically. This sort of "optical lattice" was first created in the early 1990s. When ultracold atoms are added to the lattice they are attracted or repelled from regions of strong laser intensity, depending on the colour (frequency) of the laser beams, which are kept far from an atomic absorption frequency. By varying the strength of the laser light, the experimentalists can control the positions and motions of the atoms. The result is like a juggling act, in which the balls (atoms) are kept in motion in space by precise forces exerted at just the right time.

But the juggling acts performed by the Phillips[1] and Raizen[2] groups have a twist. Imagine an identical juggler standing next to the first one. He is "air juggling"—that is, he has nothing to juggle with and is just going through the motions. The first juggler does not throw his balls to him, but even so the second juggler finds that after a time he has the balls, and the first becomes the air juggler. And then the first juggler has the balls again, and so on. This is dynamical tunnelling. The Raizen group achieved it with thousands of atoms, and the Phillips group with millions of atoms in a Bose–Einstein condensate, a form of matter in which all the atoms have the same quantum state.

But what is happening at that magical halfway point, when the balls have not completely tunnelled from one juggler to the other? At this point, the balls are in both places at once with equal probability—a feature known as quantum coherent superposition, and an essential ingredient of any approach to building quantum computers, for example. So the demonstration of dynamical tunnelling is also a demonstration of quantum coherent superposition of distinct events— all of the atoms were travelling in both directions at once. This is a fact of life in the quantum realm.

Both experimental groups worked with systems containing a degree of chaotic motion, which makes things more challenging theoretically. They did not do this deliberately—the moving optical field they created with the laser beams induces regions of classical chaos. But it raised the possibility that the process leading to the atoms going the wrong way was classical chaotic motion, rather than quantum tunnelling. Chaos is an aspect of classical systems that corresponds to extreme sensitivity to initial conditions, and often leads to rapid, seemingly random cycling between different kinds of motion. At the suggestion of Vitali Averbukh of the Technion in Israel, the Phillips group took pains to rule out the possibility that classical chaotic transport was heavily involved, thereby confirming that dynamical tunnelling was taking place.

These experiments also raise the possibility of an even newer tunnelling concept—chaos-assisted tunnelling.[6] Chaos can coexist with regions of stable, non-chaotic motion because some types of motion, called regular motion, can avoid getting mixed up in the chaotic fray. In this regime, chaos can assist tunnelling by providing a "free ride" over to another zone of regular motion once the system has tunnelled out of the first regular zone into the chaotic region.

Many previous experiments have demonstrated quantum tunnelling by individual atoms or molecules, but a nearly macroscopic system containing millions of atoms might be expected to behave more classically. Certainly near-macroscopic tunnelling has been seen before, as in the Josephson effect in superconductors or in barrier tunnelling by Bose–Einstein condensates,[7] but such observations are rare, and physicists are always hungry for more examples. From a broader perspective, these and other recent experiments demonstrate that it is possible to exert quantum control over ultracold atoms with astonishing finesse and coherence. We can look forward to a continuing stream of mind-bending examples, perhaps leading to a better understanding of the implications of quantum mechanics.

1. Hensinger, W. K. *et al. Nature* 412, 52–55 (2001).
2. Steck, D. A., Raizen, M. G. & Oskay, W. H. *Science* 5 July 2001 (10.1126/science.1061569).
3. Davis, M. J. & Heller, E. J. *J. Chem. Phys.* **75**, 246 (1981).
4. Davis, M. J. & Heller, E. J. *J. Phys. Chem.* **85**, 307 (1981).
5. Lawton, R. T. & Child, M. S. *Mol. Phys.* **44**, 709–723 (1981).
6. Tomsovic, S. & Ullmo, D. *Phys. Rev. E* **57**, 1421 (1998).
7. Anderson, B. P. & Kasevich, M. A. *Science* **282**, 1686–1689 (1998).

Many people laugh at the sport of curling. Tossing a spinning disk across ice while teammates sweep brooms in front of it? It seems a far cry from the visceral thrills and spills of skiing or ice hockey. However, like other sports, curling demonstrates the laws of motion. If you watch closely, you may notice an interesting physical phenomenon—the spinning and sliding motions of the disk, or rock, cease at the same time. You can test this yourself by tossing a spinning disk, such as a Frisbee, across a slick floor or tabletop. Also try tossing a spinning Frisbee and a non-spinning one with the same force. Which one goes farther? Why should this be true?

A team of researchers, including Zénó Farkas, Guido Bartels, Tamas Unger, and

Dietrich E. Wolf, has discovered a feedback loop that, because of friction, couples rotational and linear motion. The researchers believe that their results could have bearing on granular flows, such as grain in a silo or ice crystals in an avalanche. However, it is just as important for curlers, who must balance the spin and the forward motion of the rock so that it stops as close to the center of the goal—a series of concentric circles—as possible. —LEH

"Slip-Slidin' Away"
by David Lindley
Physical Review Focus, June 11, 2003

Enthusiasts for shuffleboard or the ancient sport of curling may have noticed a curious phenomenon: as a rotating disk skates across a surface, the spinning and sliding motions come to a halt simultaneously. In the 20 June issue of *PRL*, a team of researchers explains this oddity and shows experimental data to support their theory. The theory says that friction couples sliding and spinning motions in a way that leads to the synchronized stopping. It also predicts that a spinning disk experiences less friction and slides farther than a disk without rotation, as the team found in the lab. The researchers think this lessening of friction may occur among the grains in granular flows, such as snow cascading down a mountainside.

The direction of the frictional force always opposes the direction of motion. A disk that's both sliding and spinning has a complicated pattern of velocity across its surface: the spin causes one side to move faster than the center of the disk, while the opposite side moves slower or in the opposite direction. The velocity pattern determines the total friction on the disk, which is not simply the sum of friction calculated separately for disks that were sliding or spinning only.

This is an "almost trivial" result, says Dietrich Wolf of the University of Duisburg in Germany. "The surprising things are the consequences." Rotation reduces linear friction, and lateral motion reduces rotational friction, so that a kind of negative feedback arises. For example, if a disk is sliding fast but rotating slowly, you might expect the spinning to stop first. But the lateral motion reduces the rotational friction, so that the spinning persists longer. Wolf and his colleagues prove that the coupling of the two forms of friction is such that all combinations of sliding and spinning converge to the same endpoint, with both motions ceasing at the same time.

To test their theory, the researchers spun a plastic disk across a flat surface many times and recorded the motion with a digital camera. This was a lot of fun, says Wolf, since in Germany theoretical physicists don't normally do experiments. Even better, the results bore out their analysis. When the disk was spinning it traveled further than it did when sliding without rotation.

The researchers believe the results may apply to problems in granular flow, such as an avalanche, or grain flowing into a silo. When particles with flat facetted sides jostle and scrape past each other, the combination of linear and rotational motions may make friction less than might have been expected.

Although the new research has "interesting possibilities," says Robert Behringer of Duke University in Durham, North Carolina, figuring out its real-life significance will be hard because "granular flows are horrendously complicated [and] poorly understood." He thinks the phenomenon described by Wolf and his colleagues may be most important at the transition where dense powders begin to behave more like fluids.

One big unknown, says Leo Silbert of the University of Chicago, is whether particle surfaces remain in contact long enough for the coupling between sliding and spinning friction to influence the flow. Incorporating the new effect—"a nice, cute piece of work," Silbert calls it—into a suitable computer simulation of granular flow would help answer such practical but exceedingly difficult questions.

In 1993, Jerdone Coleman-McGhee set the Guinness World Record for stone skipping. As the cameras rolled, he threw a stone that bounced thirty-eight times on the Blanco River in Texas. One would expect that a stone, being heavier than water, would simply sink, and most stones thrown into water do just that. Even

stones that skip eventually go under. But with the right combination of angle and spin, a stone can bounce—up to thirty-eight times, evidently.

In this article, Lydéric Bocquet, a physicist from the University of Lyon, examines the physics behind how stones skip. This is not Bocquet's main line of inquiry, but in other work with Cristophe Clanet and Fabien Hersen, he has shown that the optimal angle between the stone and the water is 20 degrees. The amount of energy lost when the stone collides with the water is directly proportional to the collision time, which is at a minimum for a 20-degree angle. Thus, throwing at 20 degrees maximizes the number of bounces. —LEH

"The Physics of Stone Skipping"
by Lydéric Bocquet
American Journal of Physics, **February 2003**

I. Introduction

Nearly everyone has tried to throw a stone on a lake and count the number of bounces the stone was able to make. Of course the more, the better.[1] Our intuition gives us some empirical rules for the best throw: the best stones are flat and rather circular; one has to throw them rather fast and with a small angle with the water surface; a small kick is given with a finger to give the stone a spin. Of course these rules can be understood using the laws of physics: the crucial part of the motion is the collisional process of the stone with the water surface. The water surface exerts a reaction (lift) force on the stone, allowing it to rebound. This process is quite complex because it involves the description of the flow around the immersed stone.[2, 3] Some energy is also dissipated during a collision, so that after a few rebounds, the initial kinetic energy of the stone is fully dissipated and the stone sinks.

The purpose of this paper is to propose a simplified description of the bouncing process of a stone on water, in order to estimate the maximum number of bounces performed by the stone. This problem provides an entertaining exercise for undergraduate students, with simple explanations for empirical laws that almost everyone has experienced.

II. Basic Assumptions

Consider a flat stone, with a small thickness and a mass M. The stone is thrown over a flat water surface. The angle between the stone surface and the water plane is θ. . . . The velocity V is assumed to lie in a symmetry plane of the stone (the plane of the paper). The difficult part of the problem is, of course, to model the reaction force due to the water, which results from the flow around the stone during the stone-water contact. It is not the aim of this paper to give a detailed description of the fluid flow around the colliding stone. Rather I shall use a simplified description of the force keeping only the main ingredients of the problem. First, the velocity V of the stone is expected to be (at least initially) the order of a few meters per second. For a stone with a characteristic size a of the order of a few centimeters, the Reynolds number, defined as $Re = Va/v$, with v the kinematic viscosity ($v \sim 10^{-6}$ m^2 s^{-1} for water), is of order $Re \sim 10^5$, that is, much larger than unity.[4] In this (inertial) regime, the force due to the water on the stone is expected on dimensional grounds to be quadratic in the velocity and proportional to the apparent surface of the moving object and the mass density of the fluid.[5] Because the stone is only partially immersed in water during the collisional process, we expect the force to be proportional to the immersed surface. The force can be adequately decomposed into a component along the direction of the stone (that is, along $\mathbf{t}$) and a component perpendicular to it (that is, along $\mathbf{n}$). The latter corresponds to the lift component of the force, and the former corresponds to a friction component (of water along the object). I write the reaction force due to water, $\mathbf{F}$, as

$$\mathbf{F} = \tfrac{1}{2} C_l \rho_w V^2 S_{im} \mathbf{n} + \tfrac{1}{2} C_f \rho_w V^2 S_{im} \mathbf{t}, \qquad (1)$$

where C_l and C_f are the lift and friction coefficients, ρ_w is the mass density of water, S_{im} is the area of the immersed surface, and $\mathbf{n}$ is the unit vector normal to the stone. Note that in general, both C_l and C_f are functions of the tilt angle θ and incidence angle β, defined as the angle between velocity V and the horizontal. In the simplified analysis I will assume that both C_l and C_f are constant and independent of tilt and incidence angles.[6] This assumption is not a strong one because ricochets are generally performed with a small tilt angle, θ, and a small incidence angle, β. If one denotes the initial components of the incident velocity by V_{x0} and V_{z0} (parallel and perpendicular to the water surface, respectively), the latter assumption amounts to $V_{z0} \ll V_{x0}$.

We expect the lift force to be maximum when the object is only partially immersed due to the lack of symmetry between the two sides of the stone. Therefore, if the object reaches a depth such that it becomes completely immersed, the lift force would be greatly diminished and would probably not be able to sustain the weight of the stone anymore. For simplicity, I will assume that the lift force vanishes for completely immersed objects. The model for the force in Eq. (1) is crude, but it is expected to capture the main physical ingredients of the stone-water interaction. It might fail for lower stone velocities or larger incidence angles, where a bulge of water could be created and affect the lift and friction forces on the stone.[2] However, in this case it is expected that the stone will be strongly destabilized during the collision process and perform only a very small number of bounces. We will restrict ourselves to large initial velocities and small incidence angles, such that the number of bounces is sufficiently large.

III. Equations of Motion

Consider the collisional process, that is, the time during which the stone is partially immersed in water. I will assume in this section that the incidence angle θ between the stone and the water surface is constant during the collisional process. The validity of this assumption is considered in detail in Sec. V. The origin of time, $t=0$, corresponds to the instant when the edge of the stone reaches the water surface. During the collisional process, the equations of motion for the center of mass velocity are

$$M\frac{dV_x}{dt} = -\frac{1}{2}\,\rho_w V^2 S_{im}(C_l\sin\theta + C_f\cos\theta) \tag{2a}$$

$$M\frac{dV_z}{dt} = -Mg + \frac{1}{2}\rho_w V^2 S_{im}(C_l\cos\theta - C_f\sin\theta) \tag{2b}$$

with $V^2 = V_x^2 + V_z^2$ and g is the acceleration due to gravity. Note that in Eq. (2) the area S_{im} depends on the immersed depth and thus varies during the collisional process.

Equation (2) is nonlinear due to the V^2 terms on the righthand side, but also due to the dependence of the immersed area, S_{im}, on the height z. However, we can propose a simple approximation scheme: the magnitude of the velocity, V, is not expected to be strongly affected by the collision process (as I shall show in Sec. VI). I thus make the approximation that $V^2 \simeq V_{x0}^2 + V_{z0}^2 \simeq V_{x0}^2$ on the right-hand side of Eq. (2). The validity of this assumption requires a sufficiently high initial velocity, V_{x0}, and it might fail in the last few rebounds of a stone skip sequence.

With this approximation, Eq. (2b) decouples from Eq. (2a). I thus first focus the discussion on the equation for the height z, which is the height of the immersed edge. Note that the equation for z is equivalent to the equation of the center of mass position, Eq. (2b) because θ is assumed to be constant (see Sec. V for a detailed discussion of this point). Hence, we may identify V_z with dz/dt and Eq. (2b) yields a closed equation for the height z.

IV. Collisional Process

To solve Eq. (2b) we need to prescribe the z dependence of the immersed area S_{im}. This quantity depends on the precise shape of the stone. A natural choice is circular, which I will treat in Sec. IV B. However, it is enlightening to first consider a square shape; this shape greatly simplifies the mathematics and already contains the basic mechanisms involved.

A. A Square Stone

In this case, the immersed area is simply $S_{im}=a|z|/\sin\theta$, with a the length of one edge of the stone. The equation for z thus becomes

$$M\frac{d^2z}{dt^2}=-Mg-\frac{1}{2}\rho_w V_{x0}^2 C\frac{az}{\sin\theta} \tag{3}$$

where $C=C_l\cos\theta-C_f\sin\theta\approx C_l$, and I have used $|z|=-z$ ($z<0$). We define the characteristic frequency ω_0 as

$$\omega_0^2=\frac{C\rho_w V_{x0}^2 a}{2M\sin\theta}, \tag{4}$$

and rewrite Eq. (3) as

$$\frac{d^2z}{dt^2}+\omega_0^2 z=-g. \tag{5}$$

With the initial conditions at $t=0$ (first contact with water), $z=0$ and $\dot{z}=V_{z0}<0$, the solution of Eq. (5) is

$$z(t)=-\frac{g}{\omega_0^2}+\frac{g}{\omega_0^2}\cos\omega_0 t+\frac{V_{z0}}{\omega_0}\sin\omega_0 t. \tag{6}$$

Equation (6) characterizes the collisional process of the stone with water. After a collision time t_{coll} defined by the condition $z(t_{coll})=0$ $(t_{coll}\simeq 2\ \pi/\omega_0)$, the stone emerges totally from the water surface. It is easy to show that the maximal depth attained by the stone during the collision is

$$|z_{max}|= \frac{g}{\omega_0^2}\left[1+\sqrt{1+\left(\frac{\omega_0 V_{z0}}{g}\right)^2}\right].$$ (7)

As discussed in Sec. I, the stone will rebound if it stays only partially immersed during the collision. The rebound condition can be written as $|z_{max}|<a \sin \theta$. If we use Eqs. (7) and (4), this condition can be written after some straightforward calculations as

$$V_{x0} > V_c = \frac{\sqrt{\dfrac{4Mg}{C\rho_w a^2}}}{\sqrt{1 - \dfrac{2\tan^2\beta M}{a^3 C\rho_w \sin\theta}}}.$$ (8)

where the incidence angle β is defined as $V_{z0}/V_{x0}=\tan \beta$. Therefore, we obtain a *minimum critical velocity* for skimming. Using the typical values, $M=0.1$ kg, $a=0.1$ m, $C_l\approx C_f\approx 1$, $\rho_w=1000$ kg m^{-3}, and $\beta \sim \theta \sim 10°$, we obtain $V_c\approx 0.71$ m s$^{-1}\sim 1$ m s^{-1}.

The physical meaning of this condition is clear: it simply expresses the fact that the lift force $\frac{1}{2}C\ \rho_w V^2 a^2$ has to balance the weight of the stone Mg in order for it to bounce.

B. A Circular Stone

For a circular stone, the immersed area is a more complex function of the height z, and is given in terms of the area of a truncated circle. A simple integral calculation yields

$$S_{im}(s)=R^2[\arccos(1-s/R)$$
$$-(1-s/R\sqrt{1-(1-s/R)^2}], \qquad (9)$$

with $s=|z|/\sin\theta$ (the maximum immersed length) and $R=a/2$ is the radius of the stone.

The equation of motion for z, Eq. (2b), thus becomes nonlinear. However, it is possible to describe (at least qualitatively) the collisional process and obtain the condition for the stone to bounce.

I first introduce dimensionless variables to simplify the calculations. The dimensionless height, $\tilde{z}$, time, τ, and immersed area, A, are defined as $\tilde{z}=-z/R\sin\theta$, $\tau=\omega_0 t$, and $A(\tilde{z})=S_{im}/R^2$. (The minus sign in $\tilde{z}$ is introduced for convenience.) If we use these variables, Eq. (2b), and $V_z=dz/dt$, we obtain

$$\frac{d^2\tilde{z}}{d\tau^2}=\alpha-\frac{1}{2}A(\tilde{z}), \qquad (10)$$

with $\alpha=g/(R\omega_0^2\sin\theta)$. Equation (10) is the equation of a particle (with unit mass) in the potential $\mathcal{V}(\tilde{z})=\int(\tfrac{1}{2}A(\tilde{z})-\alpha)d\tilde{z}$. We can use standard techniques for mechanical systems to solve Eq. (10). In particular, Eq. (10) can be integrated once to give the "constant energy" condition

$$\frac{1}{2}\left(\frac{d\tilde{z}}{d\tau}\right)^2 + V(\tilde{z}) = E, \tag{11}$$

where E is the energy of the system and is given in terms of the initial conditions

$$E = \frac{1}{2}\left(\frac{d\tilde{z}}{d\tau}\right)^2\Bigg|_{\tau=0} + V(\tilde{z}=0) = \frac{1}{2}\left(V_{z0}/(R\omega_0\sin\theta)\right)^2. \tag{12}$$

The potential $\mathcal{V}(\tilde{z})$ can be calculated analytically using the expression for the immersed area S_{im} given in Eq. (9). A integral calculation gives

$$V(\tilde{z}) = \frac{1}{2}\left(\sqrt{1-(1-\tilde{z})^2}\left[\frac{2}{3} + \frac{1}{3}(1-\tilde{z})^2\right]\right.$$

$$\left. -(1-\tilde{z})\arccos(1-\tilde{z})\right) - \alpha\tilde{z} \tag{13}$$

This potential is plotted in Fig. 2 [see original article for figure] as a function of $\tilde{z}$. As a consequence of the constant energy condition, Eq. (11), $\tilde{z}$ exhibits a turning point at a maximum depth defined by $\mathcal{V}(\tilde{z}_{max}) = E$.

Here again, the condition for the stone to bounce is that this maximum depth be reached before the stone is fully immersed, that is, $|z_{max}| < 2R\sin\theta$. In terms of dimensionless variables, we obtain the condition: $\tilde{z}_{max} < 2$, with $\tilde{z}_{max}$ defined by $\mathcal{V}(\tilde{z}_{max}) = \frac{1}{2}(V_{z0}/(R\omega_0\sin\theta))^2$. This condition can be explicitly solved. Let me introduce $\tilde{z}_0$ such that $d\mathcal{V}/d\tilde{z} = 0$ at $\tilde{z} = \tilde{z}_0$: $\mathcal{V}(\tilde{z})$ is a monotonically increasing function of $\tilde{z}$ for $\tilde{z} > \tilde{z}_0$. Now it is easy to show that $\tilde{z}_{max} > z_0$ [because $\mathcal{V}(\tilde{z}_{max}) > 0$ and $\mathcal{V}(\tilde{z}_0) < 0$], and the condition $\tilde{z}_{max} < 2$ is therefore equivalent to $\mathcal{V}(\tilde{z}_{max}) < \mathcal{V}(2) = (\pi/2) - 2\alpha$, that is,

$\frac{1}{2}(V_{z0}/(R\omega_0 \sin \theta))^2 < (\pi/2) - 2g/(R\omega_0^2 \sin \theta)$. Then the condition for skimming can be rewritten (recalling that $V_{z0}/V_{x0} = \tan \beta$)

$$V_{x0} > V_c = \frac{\sqrt{\dfrac{16Mg}{\pi C \rho_w a^2}}}{\sqrt{1 - \dfrac{8M \tan^2 \beta}{\pi a^3 C \rho_w \sin \theta}}} . \tag{14}$$

Up to (slightly different) numerical factors this condition is the same as in Eq. (8) for a square stone. Note moreover, that the reasoning used for the potential $\mathcal{V}$ is quite general and can be applied to the square shape as well. This reasoning yields the same condition as Eq. (8) in this case.

Note also that for the circular stone, a simplified analysis of the motion could have been performed. First if $\tilde{z}$ remains small during the bounce of the stone, a small $\tilde{z}$ expansion of $\mathcal{V}(\tilde{z})$ is possible, yielding $\mathcal{V}(\tilde{z}) = 4\sqrt{2}/15 \tilde{z}^{5/2} - \alpha \tilde{z}$ (corresponding to a parabolic approximation for the shape of the stone near its edge). Moreover, we remark that for small V_{z0}, the energy E goes to zero, so that $\tilde{z}_{max}$ is defined in this case by $\mathcal{V}(\tilde{z}_{max}) = 0$. If we use also the previous approximation, we obtain $\tilde{z}_{max} = (15\alpha/4\sqrt{2})^{2/3}$. The condition for the stone to bounce, $\tilde{z}_{max} < 2$, therefore yields $\alpha < 16/15$. In terms of V_{x0}, this condition gives again a minimum critical velocity for skimming, defined as $V_c = \sqrt{\zeta Mg/C \rho_w a^2}$ with $\zeta = 15/4 \approx 3.75$. This result is thus close to the "exact" condition found in Eq. (14) for the $V_{z0} = 0$ case.

C. Energy Dissipation

I have so far described the rebound of the stone by analyzing its vertical motion. This analysis gave a minimum velocity for skimming which results from the balance between the weight of the stone and the lift of the force due to water. However, some energy is dissipated during the collision due to the "friction" contribution of the force (the component along x). This mechanism of dissipation leads to another minimum velocity condition, in terms of the balance between dissipation and initial kinetic energy. Only a qualitative description of the dissipation is given here.

As shown by Eq. (2), the component F_x of the reaction force in the x direction (parallel to the water surface) will decrease the velocity of the stone. Then after a few bounces, the condition for the stone to bounce, Eq. (8) or Eq. (14), will no longer be satisfied and the stone will stop. It is possible to estimate the decrease in the x component of the velocity using the equation for the center of mass position, Eq. (2a). If we multiply both sides of Eq. (2a) by V_x and integrate over a collision time, we obtain the decrease in the kinetic energy in the x direction in terms of the work of the reaction force

$$W \equiv \frac{1}{2}MV_{xf}^2 - \frac{1}{2}MV_{x0}^2 = -\int_0^{t_{coll}} F_x(t)V_x(t)dt, \qquad (15)$$

where V_{x0} and V_{xf} are the x components of the velocity before and after the collision, t_{coll} is the collision time, and $F_x = \frac{1}{2}\tilde{C}\rho_w V_x^2 S_{im}$ is the x component of the reaction force, with $\tilde{C} = C_l \sin\theta + C_f \cos\theta$.

53

A rough estimate of the right-hand side of Eq. (15) is

$$\int_0^{t_{coll}} F_x(t)V_x(t)dt \simeq V_{x0}\int_0^{t_{coll}} F_x(t)dt . \quad (16)$$

Now we have the simple relation $F_x(t)=\mu F_z(t)$, with $\mu=\tilde{C}/C$ [see Eq. (1)]. Moreover, it is expected that the average vertical force during a collision, $\langle F_z(t)\rangle=t_{coll}^{-1}\int_0^{t_{coll}}F_z(t)dt$, is the order of the weight of the stone, Mg. This point can be explicitly verified for the square stone case, using the expression of the force F_z in terms of the height $z(t)$ and Eq. (6). The final result is $\langle F_x(t)\rangle\simeq\mu M g$.[7] Moreover, as shown in the above (and in particular for the square stone, although the results remain qualitatively valid for the circular one), the collision time is given approximatively by $t_{coll}\sim 2\pi/\omega_0$. We eventually find that the loss in kinetic energy in Eq. (15) is approximatively given by

$$W\simeq-\mu MgV_{x0}\frac{2\pi}{\omega_0} =-\mu Mg\ell, \quad (17)$$

where ℓ is defined as

$$\ell=V_{x0}\frac{2\pi}{\omega_0} = 2\pi\sqrt{\frac{2M\sin\theta}{C\rho_\mu a}} \quad (18)$$

The quantity $\ell=V_x t_{coll}$ is the distance along x traversed by the stone during a collision. If the energy loss W is larger than the initial kinetic energy, the stone would be stopped during the collision. Using Eq. (15), this condition can be written explicitly as $\frac{1}{2}MV_{x0}^2>|W|=\mu Mg\ell$. We deduce that the initial velocity should be larger than the minimum velocity V_c in order to perform at least one bounce, that is,

$$V_{x0} > V_c = \sqrt{2\mu g \ell}. \tag{19}$$

If we use the same numerical values as in the previous paragraph, we obtain $\mu = 1.4$, $\ell = 13$ cm, so that $V_c \approx 2$ m s^{-1}. This criterion is more restrictive than the previous one, Eq.(14). I thus consider in the following that Eq. (19) is the criterion for the stone to skim over water.

V. Why Give the Stone a Spin?

The previous calculations assumed a constant angle θ. It is obvious that the rebound of the stone is optimized when θ is small and positive (see, for example, the value of the force constant $C = C_l \cos \theta - C_f \sin \theta$ which decreases when θ increases). Now, if after a collision, the stone is put in rotation around the y axis, that is, $\dot{\theta} \neq 0$, its orientation would change by an appreciable amount during free flight: the incidence angle θ for the next collision has little chance to still be in a favorable situation. The stone performs, say, at most one or two more collisions. There is therefore a need for a stabilizing angular motion. This is the role of the spin of the stone.

Let us denote $\dot{\phi}_0$ as the rotational velocity of the stone around the symmetry axis parallel to **n** in Fig. 1 [see original article for figure]. I neglect in the following any frictional torque on the stone (associated with rotational motion). During the collision, the reaction force due to the water is applied only to the immersed part of the stone and results in a torque applied on the stone. For simplicity, I consider only the lift part of the force. Its contribution to the torque (calculated at the center O of the stone) can be readily calculated as $M_{\text{lift}}=OP \cdot F_{\text{lift}}\mathbf{e}_y$, where $\mathbf{e}_y$ is the unit vector in the y direction in Fig. 1 and P, the point of application of the lift force, is located at the center of mass of the immersed area. This torque is in the y direction and will eventually affect the angular motion along θ. However a spin motion around $\mathbf{n}$ induces a stabilizing torque: this is the well-known gyroscopic effect.[8] The derivation of the equation of motion of the rotating object (the Euler equations) is a classic problem and is treated in standard mechanics textbooks (see, for example, Ref. 8). On the basis of these equations, it is possible to derive the stabilizing gyroscopic effect. This derivation is briefly summarized in the Appendix.

In our case, the equation for the angle θ can be written as

$$\ddot{\theta} + \omega^2(\theta-\theta_0) = \frac{M_\theta}{J_1}, \tag{20}$$

where $\omega=[(J_0-J_1)/J_1]\dot{\phi}_0$, $\dot{\phi}_0$ is the initial spin angular velocity (in the $\mathbf{n}$ direction), and J_0 and J_1 are moments of inertia in the $\mathbf{n}$ and $\mathbf{t}$ directions, respectively; θ_0 is the initial tilt angle and $M_\theta=OP \cdot F_{\text{lift}}$ is the projection of the torque due to the water flow in the y direction. Equation (20) shows that in the absence of spin motion, $\dot{\phi}_0=0$, the torque due to the lift force will initiate rotational motion of the stone in the θ direction. As discussed above, the corresponding situation is unstable. On the other hand, spin motion induces a stabilizing torque that can maintain θ around its initial value. The effect of the torque can be neglected if, after a collision with the water, the maximum amplitude of the motion of the angle θ is small: $\delta\theta = [\theta - \theta_0]_{max} \ll 1$. If we use Eq. (20), an estimate of $\delta\theta$ can be obtained by balancing the last two terms in Eq. (20), yielding $\delta\theta \sim \mathcal{M}_\theta / (J_1 \omega^2)$ [note that up to numerical factors $(J_0 - J_1)/J_1 \sim 1$ and $J_1 \sim MR^2$, with R the radius of the stone]. The order of magnitude of $\mathcal{M}_\theta$ can be obtained using the results of Sec. IV C. The average vertical force acting on the stone has been found to be the order of the weight of the stone [see the discussion after Eq. (16)]: $\langle F_z(t) \rangle \simeq Mg$. If we take $OP \sim R$, we obtain the simple result $\mathcal{M}_\theta \sim MgR$. The estimate for $\delta\theta$ follows directly as $\delta\theta \sim g/(R\omega^2)$. Therefore, the condition for θ to remain approximately constant, $\delta\theta \ll 1$, is

$$\dot{\phi}_0 \sim \omega \gg \sqrt{\frac{g}{R}} \qquad (21)$$

For a stone with a diameter of 10 cm, Eq. (21) gives $\dot{\phi}_0 \geqslant 14$ s^{-1}, corresponding to a rotational frequency larger than a few revolutions per second (~ 2 Hz). This condition is easily fulfilled in practice and corresponds approximately to what we would expect intuitively for a successful throw. Note that the condition (21) is independent of the center of mass velocity of the stone V.

VI. An Estimate for the Maximum Number of Bounces

The estimation of the maximum number of bounces is the most difficult and tentative part of the analysis because many factors can in principle slow down or destabilize the stone, some of which are extremely difficult to model (such as irregularities of the water surface and the wind). We shall assume the idealized situation described above (perfect surface, no wind, idealized reaction force) and focus on two specific factors, which appear, at least intuitively, as natural candidates for stopping the stone.

A. Slow Down of the Stone

As I have discussed in Sec. IV C, energy is dissipated during a collision and the x component of the velocity of the stone will decrease during each collision: after a few collisions, all the initial kinetic energy will be dissipated. This process can be easily formulated.

I consider a succession of N collisions. Between two collisions, the motion is parabolic (wind and air friction are neglected) and the initial x component of the velocity at the next collision is equal to the final x component of the velocity at the end of the previous collision. The important point to note is that the energy loss during one collision, Eq. (17), is independent of the velocity V_{x0} before the collision. Therefore, the velocity of the stone after N collisions obeys the relation

$$\tfrac{1}{2}MV_x^2[N] - \tfrac{1}{2}MV_x^2[0] = -N\mu Mg\ell \qquad (22)$$

so that the stone will be stopped at a collision number N_c such that the total energy loss is larger than the initial kinetic energy [similar to the argument leading to the critical velocity for skimming, V_c, in Eq. (19)]. This criterion corresponds to $V_x^2[N_c]=0$ in Eq. (22), and N_c is given accordingly by

$$N_c = \frac{V_x^2[0]}{2g\,\mu\ell}. \tag{23}$$

If we use the same typical values as before ($M=0.1$ kg, $a=0.1$ m, $C_l \approx C_f \approx 1$, $\rho_w=1000$ m^{-3}, $\beta \sim \theta \sim 10°$), we obtain $\mu \approx 1.4$ and $\ell \approx 13$ cm. We then find $N_c \approx 6$ for the initial velocity $V_{x0}=5$ m s^{-1}, $N_c \approx 17$ for $V_{x0}=8$ m s^{-1}, and $N_c \approx 38$ for $V_{x0}=12$ m s^{-1}. The latter number of bounces corresponds to the world record.[1]

It is interesting to calculate the distance between two successive collisions. As noted, the motion of the stone is parabolic out of the water: the position $\{X,Z\}$ of the particle is given by $X(t)=V_x t$, $Z(t)=-\frac{1}{2}gt^2+|V_z|t$. The next collision will occur at a distance $\Delta X=2V_x|V_z|/g$. The dependence of V_x on the number of collisions N is given by Eq.(22). On the other hand, V_z does not depend on the number of collisions because the stone rebounds "elastically" in the z direction, as follows from the analysis of the collisional process in Sec. IV (see, for example, the conservation of the energy E during the collision discussed for the circular stone). If we use Eq. (22), we obtain the simple result

$$\Delta X[N]=\Delta X_0 \sqrt{1-\frac{N}{N_c}}, \tag{24}$$

where $\Delta X_0 = 2V_{x0}|V_{z0}|/g$. Note that ΔX_0 is approximately equal to the distance between the two first ricochets, $\Delta X[N=1]$, when $N_c \gg 1$. For $V_{x0} = 8$ m s^{-1}, we obtain $\Delta X_0 \approx 2.25$ m.

Equation (24) for $\Delta X[N]$ is plotted in Fig. 3 [see original article for figure]. We remark that the decrease in the distance between two successive ricochets is first rather slow $[\Delta X[N] \simeq \Delta X_0(1-(N/2N_c))$ for $N \ll N_c$, see Eq. (24)], but strongly accelerates for the last collisions when $N \sim N_c$, due to the square root variation of $\Delta X[N]$ close to N_c. This result is in agreement with observation. Such an effect is known to specialists of stoneskipping as "pitty-pat."[1]

B. Angular Destabilization

However, there is another possible destabilizing mechanism in the collision process. As was discussed in Sec. V, the rotational stability of the stone is crucial in the collisional process. A criterion for stability has been found in the form of a minimum spin velocity of the stone. However, each collision will perturb the rotational motion and the sum of all these effects can eventually bypass the stability condition. This argument can be easily formulated. As shown above, the amplitude of the angular motion of θ is $\delta\theta \sim g/(R\omega^2)$, with $\omega \sim \dot{\phi}_0$, the (constant) spin velocity of the stone. Now assume that the destabilizing effects add, a reasonable assumption. Then, after N collisions we expect that $\Delta_N \theta \sim N\delta\theta$. The stone is completely destabilized for a collision number N_c such that $\Delta N_c \theta \sim 1$, yielding

$$N_c \sim \frac{R\dot{\phi}_0^2}{g} \ . \tag{25}$$

If we use the same numerical values as before, we obtain, for example, $N_c \simeq 5$ for a initial spin velocity $\phi_0 = 5$ rev/s and $N_c = 38$ (the world record[1]) for $\phi_0 = 14$ rev/s. Note, however, that there is a quite large uncertainty of the numerical prefactors in the above estimate of N_c, and this estimate is merely qualitative and should not be taken literally.

VII. Discussion

At the level of our description, the maximum number of bounces results from the combination of the two previous mechanisms: slow down and angular destabilization. The maximum number of bounces is therefore given by the minimum of the two previous estimates, in Eqs. (23) and (25).

The estimate N_c^{sd} obtained in Eq. (23) from the slow down of the stone depends only (quadratically) on the initial velocity of the stone: in principle, a very large number of bounces could be reached by increasing the initial velocity of the stone. But on the other hand, the angular destabilization process results in a maximum value of N_c^{spin} which is independent of the initial velocity of the stone, as indicated by Eq. (25). This shows that even if the initial velocity of the stone is very large, that is, $N_c^{sd} \gg 1$, the stone will be stopped by angular destabilization after N_c^{spin} bounces. In other words, the initial "kick" that puts the stone in rotational motion is a key factor for a good throw.

The results presented here are in agreement with our intuition for the conditions of a good throw. Some of the results are also in agreement with observations, for example, the acceleration of the number of collisions at the end of the throw (a phenomenon known as "pitty-pat" in stone skipping competitions[1]). Some easy checks of the assumptions underlying our calculations could be performed, even without any sophisticated apparatus. For example, taking pictures of the water surface after the ricochets would locate the positions of the collisions (because small waves are produced at the surface of water). A simple test of the variation of the distance between two collisions as a function of collision number, Eq. (24), would then be possible. A more ambitious project would be to design a "catapult," allowing one to throw stones with a controlled translational and spin velocity (together with the incidence angle of the stone on water). A measurement of the maximum number of bounces performed for various throw parameters would allow us to check the assumptions underlying the present simple analysis and to determine some of the parameters involved in the description (such as μ and ℓ). It would be also interesting to repeat the experiments reported in Ref. 2 using modern techniques (such as fast cameras), in order to image and analyze in particular the rebound process as a function of the throw parameters. Hopefully a better understanding of the mechanisms of stone skipping will allow someone to break the actual world record.

Acknowledgments
I thank my son Leonard for his (numerous and always renewed) perplexing questions. I thank my colleagues from the physics laboratory of the ENS Lyon, and in particular Bernard Castaing and Thierry Dauxois, for their constant interest in discussing "simple" physics problems.

Appendix
I briefly recall the derivation of Eq. (20), from the Euler equations described in Ref. 8. The latter are written as[8]

$$I_1 \frac{d\omega_1}{dt} - \omega_2 \, \omega_3 \, (I_2 - I_3) = N_1 , \tag{A1a}$$

$$I_2 \frac{d\omega_2}{dt} - \omega_1 \, \omega_3 \, (I_3 - I_1) = N_2 , \tag{A1b}$$

$$I_3 \frac{d\omega_3}{dt} - \omega_1 \, \omega_2 \, (I_1 - I_2) = N_3 . \tag{A1c}$$

In Eq. (A1), I_α, ω_α, and N_α ($\alpha = 1,2,3$) are, respectively, the moment of inertia, angular velocity, and torque along the direction of a particular principal axis, denoted as α. In our case, the direction 1 is taken along the axis perpendicular to the vectors $\mathbf{n}$ and $\mathbf{t}$, the direction 2 along $\mathbf{n}$ and the direction 3 along $\mathbf{t}$. We therefore have $\omega_1 = \dot{\theta}$, and due to the symmetry of the circular stone, $I_1 = I_3 \equiv J_1$ and $I_2 \equiv J_0$. Moreover, because only the lift component of the reaction force (along $\mathbf{n}$) is considered in the present analysis, we have $N_1 \equiv \mathcal{M}_\theta$ and $N_2 = N_3 = 0$.

Equation (A1b) yields immediately that $\dot{\omega}_2=0$. We therefore have $\omega_2=\dot{\phi}_0$, with $\dot{\phi}_0$ the initial spin velocity. Equation (A1c) can be therefore written as

$$\frac{d\omega_3}{dt}=\frac{J_1-J_0}{J_1}\dot{\phi}_0\omega_1 \, . \tag{A2}$$

If we use $\omega_1=\dot{\theta}$, Eq. (A2) can be integrated once to give

$$\omega_3=\frac{J_1-J_0}{J_1}\dot{\phi}_0(\theta-\theta_0), \tag{A3}$$

with $\theta_0=\theta(t=0)$, the initial tilt angle. The substitution of Eq. (A3) into Eq. (A1a) leads to Eq. (20).

1. The actual world record appears to be 38 rebounds (by J. Coleman-McGhee). See, for example, (http://www.stoneskipping.com) for more information on stone skipping competitions.

2. Some pictures of the bouncing process of a circular stone on water and sand can be found in C. L. Stong, "The Amateur Scientist," Sci. Am. **219**, 112–118 (1968).

3. H. R. Crane, "How things work: What can a dimple do for skipping stones?," Phys. Teach. **26**, 300–301 (1988).

4. D. J. Tritton, *Physical Fluid Dynamics*, 2nd ed. (Oxford University Press, Oxford, 1988), pp. 97–105.

5. L. D. Landau and E. M. Lifshitz, *Fluid Mechanics* (Pergamon, New York, 1959), pp. 168–175.

6. Note that the nontrivial point is to assume that C_l does not vanish and reaches a finite value in the small θ and β limit. We may invoke the finite aspect ratio (thickness over lateral size) of the object. For example, if the stone is an ellipsoid of revolution with thickness h and radius a, with $h \ll a$, we expect $C_l \sim h/a$ (Ref. 5). However the proportionality constant is expected to be sufficiently large so that the lift effect is non-negligible. This property is exemplified by water skiing. In this case, the lift force is sufficiently large to sustain the weight of a skier on small boards, while both tilt and incidence angles are close to zero.

7. It is amusing to note that the laws of friction for the stone are similar to those of solid friction. We have indeed $F_x=\mu Mg$, with $\mu=\tilde{C}/C$, independent of the

velocity and surface of the stone. Of course, the same result holds for water skiing, which is not obvious.

8. H. Goldstein, *Classical Mechanics*, 2nd ed. (Addison-Wesley, New York, 1980), pp. 203–213.

Before the bow and arrow appeared, primitive societies around the globe used the atlatl, a hand-held throwing device, to launch spearlike darts when hunting and fighting. The atlatl can launch darts at up to 100 miles per hour (161 kilometers per hour); the darts can fly hundreds of feet and pierce armor. However, the atlatl is based on the lever, a simple machine. Moving a mass with a lever requires the least effort when the mass is close to the fulcrum and the applied force is away from the fulcrum. When one throws a spear by hand, the lever arm is only the length of the palm. The atlatl, however, increases the length of the lever; the same amount of effort will hurl the spear a longer distance. The primitive societies that first developed the atlatl did not have Newton's laws of motion to guide them, but they created a very effective spear thrower. In this article, Richard A. Baugh explores those laws as he discusses a computer model of the atlatl. —LEH

"Dynamics of Spear Throwing"
by Richard A. Baugh
American Journal of Physics, **April 2003**

I. Introduction

A spear thrower enabled a stone age hunter to throw a light weight spear with greater velocity than could be obtained by hand. It consisted of a lever from 0.3 to 1.0 m long with a handgrip at one end, and a spur at the far end that engages the proximal end of the spear. In Europe the spear was definitely used in the Magdelanian period (10,000–16,000 years ago) and possibly in the Solutrean (16,000–20,000 years ago). North American spear throwers have been dated at 8,000 years. In Australia the spear thrower is popularly called a woomera, one of the many Aboriginal names for a spear thrower. In the nomenclature of North American archaeology the spear thrower is called an atlatl, a Mexican word, and the projectile is called a dart, terms that will be used in the remainder of this paper.

Atlatls were still used in the mid-twentieth century by Native Alaskans in pursuit of marine mammals and by Australian Aboriginal hunters. There has also been a resurgence of interest in atlatl marksmanship among people who are trying to relearn the skills of our stone age ancestors. The World Atlatl Association[1] holds tournaments throughout North America and Europe. Pet stores sell a "Chuckit" for throwing tennis balls to a dog.[2] This device, which works on the same principles as the atlatl, allows users to throw the ball much farther and to keep the canine saliva off their hand.

The operating principles of the atlatl are very simple. Wrist torque applied to the length of the atlatl allows wrist rotation to increase the velocity of the dart. For maximum velocity the length of the atlatl depends on the mass of the dart.

II. Objective

The main objective of this paper is to determine the relation between the dart velocity and the dimensions and weight distribution of the atlatl. Implicit in the analysis is the assumption that exactly the same human effort is used in all throws. The variation in velocity is due entirely to differences in the mass of the dart and the dimensions and weight distribution of the atlatl. A simple computer model for the process of throwing is developed. The model is sufficiently general so that it can be used to predict the velocity of a dart with arbitrary mass when thrown either by hand or with an atlatl of arbitrary dimensions. Two of the input parameters for the model, the horizontal force and wrist torque versus hand position, are derived from a high-speed video digitized recording of a person throwing a dart with an atlatl. The human effort (horizontal force and wrist torque versus hand position) is derived from a high-speed video digitizer record of a person throwing a dart with an atlatl. The other two parameters are the mass of the throwing hand and its radius of gyration. The results of applying the model to darts and atlatls of different dimensions are presented.

A model was used because a human being cannot be expected to throw with exactly the same effort time after time. In Ref. 3 experiments were done to measure the maximum distance achieved in throwing an atlatl dart. Ten throws ranged from 46.5 to 55.9 m with a mean distance thrown of 51.3 m. In Ref. 4 experiments with a weighted atlatl and one sequence of six throws achieved a mean distance of 42.6 m (140 ft) with a range of 30.5 to 54.9 m. Detailed comparative measurements of the distance thrown with an atlatl with and without an added weight were done in Ref. 5. The mean and standard deviation of the distance of 30 throws were typically 66.5 and 4.9 m. The dart velocity was measured with a radar speed gun and with a high-speed movie camera plus image digitizer. In a typical experimental run the mean dart velocity and standard deviation were 25.33 and 1.67 m/s, respectively. A different experiment yielded a mean velocity and standard deviation of 20.73 and 0.99 m/s, respectively. These experiments show that it is impossible to make identical throws even with the same atlatl and dart. To make an accurate assessment of atlatl performance, we must assume that the physical effort applied by the thrower is constant. Otherwise, the atlatl that gives the best velocity might just be the throw when the thrower was the least tired.

III. The Act of Throwing

Making a horizontal throw from a standing position involves many muscles and joints. To estimate performance, I have reduced the act of throwing to four physical parameters, a horizontal force, a wrist torque, the hand mass, and the hand radius of gyration. The horizontal force is assumed to be a function only of the horizontal position of the hand. Any dependence of the force on the speed of rotation of joints is ignored. This assumption is equivalent to saying that the contracting force of the muscles is independent of their contraction speed in the range of interest. An analysis of the experimental data shows that, with the hand initially extended in back, the thrower exerts a moderate positive (forward) force. As the hand accelerates forward, the force increases to a maximum and then decreases to zero. When the throwing hand is extended in front, the applied force becomes negative. The positive force is the result of muscular contractions, and the strong negative force at the completion of the throw is mainly the result of ligaments in the joints resisting further extension. Wrist torque is also assumed to be the result of muscular contractions. The mass and moment of inertia of the throwing hand are obtained from their physical dimensions plus the assumption that the hand density is that of water.

The idea of modeling the act of throwing by a few physical parameters, hand mass and hand radius of gyration plus force and wrist torque, as measurable functions of hand position was inspired by the work of Paul Klopsteg on the physics of bows and arrows.[6] He characterized the operation of a bow by two parameters; the available energy stored in the bow limbs and the virtual mass of the bow limbs. The virtual mass is derived from data on arrow kinetic energy versus arrow mass. In his simple model the fraction of the available energy stored in the bow limbs that is imparted

to an arrow is a function only of the arrow mass: the efficiency = arrow mass/(arrow mass + virtual mass). For a given bow, the concepts of available energy and virtual mass of the bow make it easy to calculate the velocity for arrows of any mass.

Cotterell and Kamminga applied Klopsteg's concept of virtual mass to hand thrown and atlatl thrown spears.[7] They used a much more detailed model for throwing, which included the mass and moment of inertia of the forearm and hand. They also assumed that the angular velocities of the elbow and wrist joints are fixed and independent of the masses being moved. This independence is in contrast with the model presented here, which assumes a predetermined force and torque.

The thrower simultaneously applies a force and wrist torque. The horizontal component of force causes horizontal acceleration. It also causes angular acceleration when the force is not collinear with the center of mass. Additional angular acceleration comes from the wrist torque and the vertical component of force.

Wrist torque is also important with a hand-thrown projectile. A baseball pitcher, throwing off the tips of his fingers, applies wrist rotation over a lever arm extending from his wrist joint to his fingertips, approximately 16 to 20 cm. With a hand-thrown spear, the wrist rotation is applied to a lever, wrist joint to palm, which is only about 10 cm long. The use of an atlatl allows the optimization of the lever length for the dart mass and physical limitations of the thrower. The model treats hand thrown and atlatl thrown darts as essentially the same, and only the length and mass of the lever arm are different. The

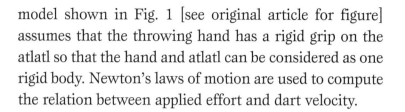

model shown in Fig. 1 [see original article for figure] assumes that the throwing hand has a rigid grip on the atlatl so that the hand and atlatl can be considered as one rigid body. Newton's laws of motion are used to compute the relation between applied effort and dart velocity.

IV. The Experiment

Position versus time data was obtained with a high-speed video digitizer. Small tabs of reflecting tape were placed on the atlatl near the hand and the spur and on the dart at the middle, rear, and front ends to reflect light into the digitizer. Several throws were made to verify that the equipment was working correctly. In the final throw the horizontal and vertical positions of all five spots were measured every 5/1000 s and recorded for later computer analysis. Figure 2 [see original article for figure] shows the atlatl position every 0.02 s. The horizontal and vertical scales are both in meters. The initial position is on the left, the final on the right.

Table I summarizes the physical dimensions of the atlatl, dart, and equivalent mass, and the radius of gyration of the hand used in the experiment [see original article for table]. From the measured positions versus the time and the masses and dimensions of the equipment, we can calculate the force and torque applied by the thrower. The thrower, an athletic 50 year old man, launched the dart with a "moderate" effort, the sort of throw that one would use for accuracy rather than trying for maximum distance. The following assumptions were made to analyze the data: (a) The horizontal velocity of the dart is the quantity of interest. (b) The hand and atlatl are considered to be one rigid entity with a mass, center of mass, and rotational moment of inertia. (c) The dart is sufficiently long that the atlatl spur, the part of the atlatl which engages the dart, can only apply a horizontal force to the rear end of the dart. (d) The vertical components of force are only included in the torque because their only effect is to cause angular acceleration of the atlatl.

The applied hand force and the reaction force involved in accelerating the dart act upon the center of mass of the hand-atlatl system,

$$M\frac{d^2x}{dt^2}=F(x_h)-M_d\frac{d^2x_d}{dt^2} \,,\qquad(1)$$

where M is the sum of the hand mass, atlatl mass, and any weight added to the atlatl, x is the position of the center of mass of the hand plus atlatl plus any weight added to the atlatl, M_d is the mass of the dart, $F(x_h)$ is the applied horizontal force, and x_d is the horizontal position of the dart. The estimates for the acceleration, a_i, are derived from the second differences of the experimentally obtained position, where i is the time index,

$$a_x(i)=\frac{(x_{i+1}-2x_i+x_{i-1})}{\Delta t^2} \,,\qquad(2)$$

where Δt is the time interval between measurements. The final step is to fit a continuous mathematical function to the experimentally determined force,

$$F(x_h)=900[(x_h+0.05)^{1.5}](0.802-x_h) \,,\qquad(3)$$

where x_h is the hand position and the constants were chosen to give the least mean squared error compared with the experimental data. Initially $x_h = 0$.

The relation between the angular acceleration, wrist torque, and the hand force and reaction force from accelerating the dart is

$$I_{ha}\frac{d^2}{dt^2}\phi = T(x_h) - F(x_h)L_{ch}\sin(\phi)$$

$$-M_d\frac{d^2}{dt^2}x_d L_{cs}\sin(\phi), \qquad (4)$$

where ϕ is the rotation angle of the atlatl relative to horizontal, I_{ha} is the moment of inertia of the hand–atlatl system about the center of mass, $T(x_h)$ is the applied wrist torque, L_{ch} is the distance from center of mass to the hand, and L_{cs} is the distance from the center of mass to the atlatl spur. The continuous function used to fit the experimental torque data is

$$T(x_h) = 150(x_h^{3.6})(1.07 - x_h). \qquad (5)$$

An analysis of the experimental data showed that the maximum force that Baker applied during the throw, 110 N (25 lbs), was about half of the 178 N he could apply statically with a moderate effort to a spring scale. Furthermore, the force started very small at about 8 N, built up gradually to 110 N, and gradually dropped to zero with his hand almost at maximum extension in front and then more rapidly reversed direction as he reached maximum extension at the end of the throw. At maximum forward extension, the reverse directed force was -280 N. The applied wrist torque built up gradually from zero to its maximum value of 18 N m at maximum extension, just before the dart left the atlatl.

Figures 3 and 4 are the experimentally derived force and torque versus hand position [see original article for figures]. The noise in the results is primarily due to imperfect spatial resolution in the video digitizer. Also plotted in Figs. 3 and 4 are the results of the models used to represent the force and torque versus hand position.

V. Going from Force to Velocity

The hand force was derived from the acceleration data and then, knowing the applied force, the torque was derived from the angular acceleration in a straightforward manner. The reverse process, deriving the position and velocity from the applied force and torque, is more difficult. In order to do this it is instructive to write down the Lagrangian for this system. An initial attempt used x, the horizontal position of the center of mass, and ϕ, the angle of the atlatl, as coordinates. The kinetic energy, expressed in terms of those coordinates and their time derivatives, is

$$KE_1 = \tfrac{1}{2}\{M_{ha}v_x^2 + I_{ha}\omega^2 + M_d[v_x + L_{cs}\,\omega\,\sin(\phi)]^2\}. \qquad (6)$$

Equation (6) contains a term, $v_x\omega$, that complicates the analysis. A simple expedient eliminates this term. Figure 5 [see original article for figure] shows a massless spring with spring constant k inserted between the atlatl spur and the proximal end of the dart. In addition

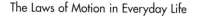
to the two original coordinates x and ϕ, a third, x_d, the horizontal position of the proximal end of the dart, is required. Then

$$KE = \tfrac{1}{2}\left(M_{ha}v_x^2 + I_{ha}\omega^2 + M_d v_d^2\right),\tag{7}$$

and the potential is

$$V = -\int_0^{x_h} F(u)\,du - \int_0^{\varphi} T(u)\,du$$

$$+\tfrac{1}{2}k[x_d - (x - L_{cs}\cos(\phi))]^2.\tag{8}$$

We see that there are no terms in the kinetic energy involving the product of one velocity with another.

Initially x_h and $\phi = 0$. The first term in Eq. (8) is integrated over the hand position, which is initially at C_m. The three equations of motion are then

$$M_{ha}\frac{d^2x}{dt^2} = F(x + L_{ch}\cos(\phi)) + k[x_d - (x - L_{cs}\cos(\phi))]\tag{9}$$

for the center of mass,

$$I_{ha}\frac{d^2\phi}{dt^2} = T(x + L_{ch}\cos(\phi)) - F(x + L_{ch}\cos(\phi))$$

$$\times L_{ch}\sin(\phi) - k(x - L_{cs}\cos(\phi) - xd)L_{cs}\sin(\phi)\tag{10}$$

for the atlatl rotation, and

$$M_d\frac{d^2x_d}{dt^2} = k(x - L_{cs}\cos(\phi) - x_d)\tag{11}$$

for the dart position.

An additional advantage of adding the spring is that it facilitates the analysis of flexibility in the atlatl. A rigid atlatl is represented by a large spring constant and a more flexible atlatl by a smaller spring constant. The Runge–Kutta differential equation solver in Mathcad readily solves these equations. As a check, the parameters of the system used in the experiment were entered in the model. Figure 6 [see original article for figure] shows the horizontal velocity of the distal end of the spring versus time as measured and as computed from the model. The dart separates from the spring immediately after the maximum velocity occurs and continues on with that velocity.

VI. Results of Computer Model

The objectives of the model are to quantify the relationship between dart velocity, dart mass, and atlatl dimensions and to analyze the effect of flexibility in the atlatl. The selection of the atlatl and dart dimensions to use in the model is determined by the archaeological and ethnographic records and by the practice of contemporary users of the atlatl. In Ref. 8, 33 hand thrown spears and 293 atlatl darts from Australia were examined, but the dimensions of the atlatls used with the darts were not mentioned. The mean mass of the hand thrown spears was 740 g with a fairly uniform distribution from 100 to 1350 g. The darts had a mean mass of 246 g with a range of 50 to 850 g; a fraction 58/293 had masses between 50 and 100 g. Reference 9 discusses examples of Australian spear throwers ranging from 0.51 to 1.17 m long and Inuit (Eskimo) spear throwers about 0.50 m long. A

Great Basin atlatl dart with a mass of 57 g has been repli-cated and Great Basin atlatls lengths ranging from 0.45 to 0.71 m have been cited.[10] The 7 darts considered in Ref. 4 ranged from 52 to 91 g with a mean of 73, the atlatls ranged from 0.48 to 0.57 m long with a weight from 72 to 82 g, and an added weight of 40 g. The dimensions of an atlatl and dart manufactured by BPS Engineering are cited in Table I[11] [see original article for table]. We did calculations for 50, 73, 150, and 250 g darts as represen-tative of the lighter Aboriginal darts, the BPS dart, and replicas in Refs. 4 and 10. The different atlatls used in the initial model are rigid and have mass proportional to length: $M_a = 0.082L_a/0.61 = 0.134$ kg/m. The quantities L_{ch}, I_{ch}, and M_a, the distance from center of mass to hand, moment of inertia, and atlatl mass as a function of atlatl length, are defined in the Appendix.

Surprisingly, the simulation implies that the atlatl length for maximum velocity is much shorter than what is observed in actual practice. There could be several reasons for this. The initial assumption that the human effort (force and torque) is independent of the masses involved may not be valid. The force and torque profiles versus hand position may depend on the rate of muscle contraction. It is very difficult to hold a very long dart with a very short atlatl. And the difference in velocity between a long atlatl and a short one may be too small to be perceptible.

VII. Atlatl Weights

The archaeological record in North America is unusual in that many examples of atlatls have been found with a weight attached near the center. One conjecture is that this weight enabled the hunter to throw with greater velocity. Another hypothesis is that in the final portion of the throw with the throwing hand extended, the hand force strongly negative, and the atlatl nearly vertical, that the negative hand force causes an additional positive torque on the atlatl and increases the terminal velocity of the dart. This hypothetical increase would be more or less negated by reduced horizontal acceleration due to the additional weight. The model is ideally suited to testing this hypothesis. Weights of 50, 78, and 120 g were placed at 0, 0.1, 0.2, 0.3, or 0.4 m from the proximal end of a 0.5 m atlatl and the velocity computed for a 50 g dart. Adding a weight to the atlatl reduced the velocity but not by very much.

VIII. Atlatl Flexibility

Mechanical energy can be stored in the flexing of an elastic structure such as a bow limb, a rubber band, a clock spring, or an atlatl. There are many examples in nature and in simple machinery where mechanical energy storage is used to increase the efficiency of energy transfer from a heavy, slow moving object to a lighter object, a phenomenon called resonant energy transfer. One example is the crack of a whip. The kinetic energy of the heavy whip handle is transferred efficiently along one section of the tapered whip to the next. At the tip the velocity exceeds the speed of sound and we hear a sonic boom. The flexibility of the atlatl has the potential to make a significant increase in the dart velocity because at the instant the dart leaves the spur, there is still some kinetic energy remaining in the atlatl. This possibility was explored by reducing the stiffness of the spring connecting the atlatl spur and the dart . . . The velocity is plotted versus spring deflection distance. The spring deflection is proportional to the force applied to the dart and is inversely proportional to the spring constant. The velocity is plotted for a range of spring deflections that represents actual practice by contemporary users of atlatl. Note that for the range examined the dependence of velocity on spring deflection is a monotonically increasing function with no sharp resonance. The simple model is probably not valid for spring deflections greater than 20 % of the atlatl length.

IX. Conclusions

A high-speed video digitizer was used to capture the coordinates of an atlatl every 0.005 s during a throw. A model of the act of throwing based on this experimental data was then developed. The model was used to predict the behavior of atlatls of arbitrary dimensions used with different projectile masses. The model is sufficiently general that it can also be used for hand thrown spears. A quantitative estimate of the importance of flexibility in the atlatl was presented.

This human/machine system provides an excellent opportunity for additional research. Only one data set was used because there was a 200 mile round trip between my home and the laboratory where the experiment was done. A faster method for gathering velocity versus time data would be very valuable for testing the hypothesis that applied force and torque are independent of the load or velocity. One method would be to attach a low mass sound source to the atlatl spur and use the Doppler shift to measure velocity versus time.[12] Two sound sources with different frequencies could be attached to different places on the atlatl and enable simultaneous measurements of the velocity and angular velocity. The assumption that force and torque depend only on hand position should be verified by throwing with different masses. In practice the force on the dart is collinear with the trajectory only on the average and consequently some rotational moment is applied to the dart. This moment can be canceled by making the oscillation period of the dart commensurate with the time it takes to throw. Another question that can be investigated is the extent to which small angular variations in throwing effort cause larger changes in the dart trajectory.

Acknowledgments

Professor Mont Hubbard of the Mechanical Engineering Department at the University of California at Davis provided the high speed video digitizer and Dan Reid, a mechanical engineering undergraduate, helped us use it. Tim Baker did the throwing. Bob Perkins of BPS Engineering made the atlatl and dart.

Appendix: The Moment of Inertia of the Hand Plus Atlatl

The atlatl used to obtain the experimental data consists of a small diameter rod with constant density per unit length with a weight added near the middle. Its dimensions plus that of the throwing hand are given in Table

I [see original article for table]. The center of mass is located at a distance

$$C_m = \frac{(0.5 L_a M_a + L_w M_w)}{(M_a + M_h + M_w)} \tag{A1}$$

from the proximal end, and the moment of inertia about the center of mass is

$$I_{ha} = \frac{1}{12} M_a L_a^2 + M_a \left(\frac{L_a}{2} - C_m\right)^2 + M_h R_h^2 + M_h C_m^2$$
$$+ M_w (L_w - C_m)^2. \tag{A2}$$

For atlatls of arbitrary length, the mass is assumed to be proportional to the length

$$M_a = 0.134 L_a \text{ kg/m.} \tag{A3}$$

References

1. The World Atlatl Association, (http//www.worldatlatl.org/).
2. A Web site that advertises the Chuckit, a device for throwing tennis balls, is (http://www.caninehardware.com/products–chuckits.html).
3. C. Howard, "The Atlatl: Function and performance," Am. Antiq. **39**, 102–104 (1974).
4. M. W. Hill, "The atlatl or throwing stick. A recent study of atlatls in use with darts of various sizes," Tenn. Archaeol. Soc. **IV** (4), 37–44 (1948).
5. Anan Raymond, "Experiments in the function and performance of the weighted atlatl," World Archaeol. **18** (2), 153–177 (1986).
6. P. E. Klopsteg, "Physics of bows and arrows," Am. J. Phys. **11**, 175–180 (1943).
7. Brian Cotterell and Johan Kamminga, *Mechanics of Pre-industrial Technology* (Cambridge U. P., Cambridge, 1992), Chap. 7.
8. J. L. Palter, "Design and construction of Australian spear thrower projectiles and hand thrown spears," Archaeol. Phys. Anthropol. Oceania **12**, 161–172 (1977).
9. George C. Stone, *A Glossary of the Construction, Decoration and Use of Arms and Armor in all Countries and in all Times* (Jack Brussel, New York, 1934).
10. T. R. Hester, M. P. Mildner, and L. Spencer, *Great Basin Atlatl Studies* (Ballena, Ramona, CA, 1974), a master's thesis in archaeology on the atlatls and projectiles used in this region.

11. (http://www.atlatl.com/) the Web site for BPS Engineering, the company that made the atlatl and dart used in the experiment.

12. T. J. Bensky, "Computer sound card assisted measurements of the acoustic Doppler effect for accelerated and unaccelerated sound sources," Am. J. Phys. **69**, 1231–1236 (2001).

The Laws of Motion and the Animal World

3

The word "catapult" generally conjures images of an invading army besieging a castle, using the huge equipment to hurl rocks and other projectiles against fortified defenses in an attempt to weaken or breach them. Such catapults are simply giant springs, one of the many applications of physics in warfare. Twisted ropes or bent wood store potential energy. When released, the arm of the catapult moves forward quite fast, flinging the rock resting in the bowl toward the target.

Although modern warfare relies on guns and bombs, catapults can still be found today in the animal kingdom. The following article describes the tongue of a chameleon, which acts like a catapult in order to achieve accelerations of 500 m s^{-2}, or 51g (one "g" is the gravitational force exerted on a body at rest and used to indicate the force to which a body is subjected when accelerated). Space shuttle astronauts experience only 3g during liftoff, so that's a very powerful tongue. —LEH

"Power at the Tip of the Tongue"
by Ulrike K. Müller and Sander Kranenbarg
Science, April 9, 2004

Chameleons launch their tongues at unsuspecting insects at speeds of 26 body lengths per second. They can catch insect prey located up to 1.5 body lengths away within a tenth of a second. This impressive performance drove biologists to formulate far-fetched explanations, such as that the chameleon's tongue is "erected" through an increase in blood pressure or inflated by the lungs like a party favor. More recent theories invoke the action of the tongue's large accelerator muscle [see [1] for a review]. In a recent issue of the *Proceedings of the Royal Society of London*, de Groot and van Leeuwen[1] report that the chameleon's tongue is projected with more power than can be supplied by any known muscle. These investigators reveal that the chameleon's tongue is, in fact, powered by an ingenious catapult system.

The secret to prey evading capture or to predators capturing prey is rapid acceleration. But there are limitations to how fast muscles can contract. To achieve speeds beyond these limitations, for example, the legs of a jumping kangaroo rat act like levers, which turn slow but forceful muscle contractions into much faster movements. Long levers, however, require enormous forces, which the muscles are required to deliver quickly for the animal to escape. Limited by its muscle power, a jumping kangaroo rat reaches an acceleration of a mere 19g (humans tend to faint at accelerations above 10g).[2] To reach even higher speeds and accelerations, animals have developed catapults to increase their power output. A catapult enables muscles to slowly load an elastic energy store. The catapult then releases this energy very quickly, providing much higher speeds than could be delivered by the muscle directly. Froghoppers (also known as spittlebugs) hold the current record, accelerating at 408g when they catapult themselves into the air.[3]

The chameleon's tongue accelerates at 500 m s^{-2} (51g) to speeds of up to 6 m s^{-1}.[1] If projection of the chameleon's tongue were powered directly by the accelerator muscle, then this muscle would need to generate peak powers of up to 3000 W per kg of muscle. This value is considerably higher than any values reported so far for vertebrate muscle[4] and exceeds the chameleon's muscle capacity by almost an order of magnitude.[1] This suggested to de Groot and van Leeuwen that the chameleon's tongue must achieve acceleration in some other way, perhaps by acting as a catapult.

Any catapult requires a stiff frame, an energy store, and a power supply. By carefully dissecting the tongues of several chameleons, the authors were able to show that the skeleton of the tongue—a long, stiff rod of cartilage—provides the frame of the catapult. The elastic energy is stored in nested sheaths of collagen tissue that surround the tongue skeleton. These, in turn, are surrounded by the accelerator muscle. When this muscle is activated it contracts radially and, as muscle is incompressible, it lengthens along the skeleton. The elongating muscle stretches the attached helical collagen fibers, loading them with elastic energy. When the tongue catapults, the stretched collagen tissue slides off the tongue skeleton. Only at the tip of the skeleton can these sheaths relax radially, and, as each annular section squeezes over the taper, it forces the tongue forward. This "sliding spring" mechanism converts the stored elastic energy into kinetic energy and the tongue is launched forward at a dizzying speed.

The investigators demonstrate that the chameleon's catapult does not require a latch to fire. The tongue-retractor complex prevents the elongating accelerator muscle from sliding backward while the front end of the muscle moves closer and closer to the tip of the tongue bone. The catapult is released at the moment when the muscle's most distal end slips off the tongue skeleton. This built-in trigger adds no extra moving parts or controls to the catapult. All it requires is a tongue skeleton that tapers off only at the very tip, so that the muscle can build up enough elastic energy before it begins sliding off.

The chameleon's "sliding spring" is remarkably compact, efficient, and easy to control. Conventional catapults store tensile energy in a rope or tendon that is loaded and unloaded along the same path. By using a collagen tube rather than a tendon, the chameleon can load the spring by global longitudinal tension but release its energy by local radial contraction. This asymmetric loading-and-unloading pattern has two advantages. First, the loading structure (the accelerator muscle) and the energy-storage structure (the collagen tube) can be arranged concentrically. The tongue projector is thus compact, with admirably few moving parts or force transducers that would increase wear and reduce efficiency.

Second, the sliding spring releases its elastic energy gradually as consecutive portions of the collagen tube slide off the tongue tip. Sudden acceleration is particularly unfavorable when shooting soft projectiles such as a tongue: Much energy can be lost in internal deformations and vibrations. Salamanders of the genus Hydromantes, which also project their tongue ballistically,[5] avoid this problem by shooting out the stiff tongue skeleton together with the tongue itself.

In a primitive catapult, the force and acceleration are directly proportional to the extension of the spring (Hooke's law) and, therefore, are greatest at the moment of release. Conventional engineering designs, such as the compound bow, modify these characteristics by means of non-Hookean springs and dynamic levers. In a sliding-spring catapult,[1] the course of energy release is determined in a radically different way. Its components are arranged in parallel along an axis that corresponds to the time course of the driving force. Thus, spatial modulation of elastic loading along this axis programs the time course of the launching force. The chameleon can presumably "tune" the launch of its tongue by changing muscle recruitment (on the animal's time scale), or the muscle's shape and size (on an evolutionary time scale), without having to "invent" new lever elements or change the mechanical properties of existing elements. The extraordinary degree of functional integration in the chameleon's tongue, so unlike the modular designs of mechanical engineers, might explain how the chameleon has hidden its secret catapult from biologists for so long.

References

1. J. H. de Groot, J. L. van Leeuwen, *Proc. R. Soc. London Ser. B* 271, 761 (2004).
2. A. A. Biewener, R. Blickhan, *J. Exp. Biol.* 140, 243 (1988).
3. M. Burrows, *Nature* 424, 509 (2003).
4. G. N. Askew, R. L. Marsh, *J. Exp. Biol.* 204, 3587 (2001).
5. S. M. Deban et al., *Nature* 389, 27 (1997).

The authors are in the Experimental Zoology Group, Wageningen University, 6709 PG Wageningen, Netherlands. E-mail: ulrike.muller@wur.nl

Reprinted with permission from Müller , Ulrike K. and Sander Kranenbarg. "Power at the Tip of the Tongue," *Science* 304:217–219 (2004). © 2004 AAAS.

Have you ever wondered why a cat always lands on its feet after falling? Surprisingly, the same physical principles behind the cat's acrobatics can also be observed in molecules of carbon dioxide, or CO_2. Physics students are familiar with both masses on springs and pendulums. One can also create a spring pendulum—a mass on a spring that swings side to side like a pendulum as well as contracts and expands. Many molecules act like spring pendulums, including CO_2. All molecules vibrate, which means that the bonds between atoms can stretch and contract, and that the bonds can swing so that the angles between them change. In CO_2, the carbon atom is the fixed point, whereas the oxygen atoms and the C–O bonds are the masses and springs. The phenomenon CO_2 shares with the falling cat is that they each appear to temporarily gain *angular momentum where none previously existed. By determining the conditions under which this occurs, the following article brings classical, Newtonian physics one step closer to quantum mechanics. —LEH*

"Nonlinear Dynamics: Quantizing the Classical Cat"
by Ian Stewart
Nature, August 12, 2004

A central problem in modern physics is to find effective methods for quantizing classical dynamical systems— modifying the classical equations to incorporate the effects of quantum mechanics. One of the main obstacles is the disparity between the linearity of quantum theory and the nonlinearity of classical dynamics. Taking a big step forward, R. H. Cushman *et al.* have analysed a quantum version of the spring pendulum, whose resonant state was first discussed by Enrico Fermi and which is a standard model for the carbon dioxide molecule (*Phys. Rev. Lett.* **93**, 024302; 2004).

Cushman *et al.* show that when this system is quantized, the allowed states, or eigenstates, fail to form a perfect lattice, contrary to simpler examples. Instead, the lattice has a defect, a point at which the regular lattice structure is destroyed. They show that this defect can be understood in terms of an important classical phenomenon known as monodromy. A quantum-mechanical cliché is Schrödinger's cat, whose role is to dramatize the superposition of quantum states by being both alive and dead. Classical mechanics now introduces a second cat, which dramatizes monodromy through its ability always to land on its feet. The work affords important new insights into the general problem of quantization, as well as being a beautiful example of the relation between nonlinear dynamics and quantum theory.

The underlying classical model here is the swing–spring, a mass suspended from a fixed point by a spring. The spring is free to swing like a pendulum in any vertical plane through the fixed point, and it can also oscillate along its length by expanding and contracting. The Fermi resonance occurs when the spring frequency is twice the swing frequency. The same resonance occurs in a simplified model of the two main classical vibrational modes of the carbon dioxide molecule, and the first mathematical analysis of the swing–spring was inspired by this model.

Using a modern technique of analysis known as reduction, which exploits the rotational symmetry of a system, Cushman *et al.* show that this particular resonance has a curious implication, which manifests itself physically as a switching phenomenon. Start with the spring oscillating vertically but in a slightly unstable state. The vertical "spring mode" motion quickly becomes a "swing mode" oscillation, just like a clock pendulum swinging in some vertical plane. However, this swing state is transient and the system returns once more to its spring mode, then back to a swing mode, and so on indefinitely. The surprise is that the successive planes in which it swings are different at each stage.

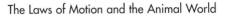

Moreover, the angle through which the swing plane turns, from one occurrence to the next, depends sensitively on the amplitude of the original spring mode.

The apparent paradox here is that the initial state has zero angular momentum—the net spin about the vertical axis is zero. Yet the swing state rotates from one instance to the next. Analogously, a falling cat that starts upside down has no angular momentum about its own longitudinal axis, yet it can invert itself, apparently spinning about that axis. The resolution of the paradox, for a cat, is that the animal changes its shape by moving its paws and tail in a particular way. At each stage of the motion, angular momentum remains zero and is thus conserved, but the overall effect of the shape changes is to invert the cat. The final upright state also has zero angular momentum, so there is no contradiction of conservation. This effect is known as the "geometric phase," or monodromy, and is important in many areas of physics and mathematics.

The central topic of the paper is this: how does monodromy show up when the system is quantized? The answer, obtained in the specific context of the carbon dioxide molecule, is both elegant and remarkable.

A molecule of carbon dioxide can be modelled classically as a central carbon atom, attached symmetrically by identical springs to two oxygen atoms, with the springs inclined at an obtuse angle. The molecule has three main vibrational modes. The two most important modes are symmetric stretching, where both springs change their lengths in synchrony, and bending, where the angle between the two springs oscillates. These modes are analogous to the spring and swing modes of a swing–spring. The third main mode, asymmetric stretching, occurs when the two springs oscillate out of phase with each other, and it can be removed from consideration by averaging over a vibrational cycle. The result is a "reduced Hamiltonian," or energy function, which is simpler than the exact Hamiltonian but is still a good model.

The quantum energy–momentum lattice of the molecule consists of the eigenstates of this Hamiltonian, that is, the pure vibrational modes. For a fixed energy, these modes correspond to two classical "constants of motion"—angular momentum and a quantity related to the rotational symmetry. The eigenstates can be characterized by two quantum numbers, which are integers, so these eigenstates form a regular planar lattice like a chessboard.

However, there is an extra quantum number, related to another classical variable, called the "action." The new phenomenon here is that, because of monodromy, the action is defined only locally and cannot be consistently extended across the entire lattice. For fixed quantum numbers in the lattice, this additional quantum number can take on infinitely many values, at equally spaced points at right angles to the chessboard. The simplest structure of this kind is a three-dimensional cubic lattice—an infinite stack of chessboards, vertically above each other. Monodromy implies that the totality of all sets of quantum numbers does not form a cubic lattice. Instead, it has a single topological defect where the regularity of the lattice structure breaks down.

This analysis is important because it suggests, and supports, a general principle. The most significant features of the quantum-mechanical description of a classical system occur at its singularities. The singularities introduce defects into the ensemble of quantum eigenstates, but they also organize the structure of those defects. Everywhere else, quantization works just as in previous, simpler examples. The authors suggest several directions for future progress, mostly to develop the growing use of nonlinear dynamics in the understanding of quantization. But the most tantalizing is the possibility of detecting quantum monodromy experimentally. Maybe we will soon be able to see how Schrödinger's cat turns itself upside down.

Humans cannot walk on water, at least not without technological or divine intervention. However, water striders, also known as skaters or Jesus bugs, seem to glide effortlessly across the surface of a pond or lake. Newton's third law states that for every action there must be an equal and opposite reaction. Thus, for an object to move forward, it must push backward on something. The water strider's legs obviously push against the surface of the water, but until now researchers have not understood just how this creates enough momentum to propel the

insects forward, as pushing against a fluid is very different from walking on solid ground.

This article discusses research by David L. Hu, Brian Chan, and John W. M. Bush that demonstrates that researchers had not been looking deep enough for an explanation. The backward momentum is actually beneath the water surface in vortices — limited areas in which the fluid moves in a spiral motion. This work has enabled the researchers to develop a robotic water strider that walks on water like its biological counterparts. —LEH

"Animal Locomotion: How to Walk on Water"
by Michael Dickinson
Nature, August 7, 2003

A glance at the surface of a pond reveals one of the more delightful images of summer: the shimmering ripples made by the graceful strokes of water striders. Water striders are insects that are adapted for locomotion and foraging on top of still water. Long hairy legs keep these animals afloat, but how do they glide so effortlessly across the surface? Models of water-strider locomotion have proposed that the animals move forwards by creating surface waves that carry momentum backwards. An elegant study by Hu, Chan and Bush[1] . . . shows that this view is, quite literally, superficial. Like the oars of a rowing-boat, a water strider's legs create swirling vortices that carry momentum *beneath* the surface of

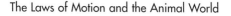

the water. It is the rearwards motion of these vortices, and not the surface waves, that propels the animal forwards. This insight solves a paradox related to the motion of juvenile water striders, and helps to form a more cohesive picture of animal locomotion.

Much of animal locomotion distils down to a simple application of Newton's third law: to move forwards, animals must push something backwards.[2] Just what that something is depends on the form of locomotion. Large terrestrial animals push against the solid ground, creating reaction forces in the opposite direction. The situation is a bit more complicated for swimming and flying animals, which must push against a fluid (from a physical standpoint, both air and water are fluids). As a fin or wing flaps, the fluid yields to form a pattern of swirling vortices. In some cases, the energy transmitted by an animal to the fluid in one stroke takes the form of a discrete vortex: a doughnut-shaped structure like a smoke ring. Birds,[3] bats,[4] insects[5] and fish[6] have all been shown to create a series of vortices as they move, although the precise arrangement may be complex and notoriously difficult to quantify. By carefully measuring the size, strength and velocity of the vortices generated during each stroke, it is theoretically possible to reconstruct the average force with which an animal propels itself through the air or water.[7, 8]

But what about tiny creatures such as water striders, that live between air and water? What do they push backwards to move forwards, and how do they stay afloat in the first place? Resting statically on the water surface poses no great problem to a small organism.[9]

Surface-tension forces at an air–water interface result from the mutual attraction of water molecules through hydrogen bonds. As the wax-covered, hairy legs of an insect dimple the water downwards, these surface-tension forces push the animal upwards. Whereas the total upward force is proportional to the perimeter of contact, which increases linearly with body size, the mass of the animal that must be supported by the tension forces increases proportionally to the cube of its body length. Thus, whereas a small water strider can easily stand atop water, larger insects need proportionally longer legs to ensure that they can rest on the surface with suitable safety. As documented by Hu *et al.*,[1] this requirement for ever-longer legs limits the maximum size of a water strider to about 25 centimetres.

Understanding how water striders transfer momentum to move forwards is much tougher. One possible explanation is that they transfer momentum backwards in the tiny surface ripples created as they sweep their legs. Unlike the more familiar waves of the open ocean that are dominated by gravity, the tiny ripples generated by the legs of water striders are termed capillary waves and are dominated by surface tension. To generate a capillary wave, an insect leg (or any object, for that matter) must move faster than about 25 cm s^{-1}—the minimum speed at which any surface wave can travel. Exceeding this speed is no problem for the long legs of water-strider adults, but is beyond the capacity of the juveniles. If juvenile water striders cannot move the tips of their legs fast enough to create the surface waves, how do they propel themselves? This enigma was

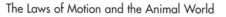

identified by Mark Denny,[9] and is known to water-strider enthusiasts as Denny's paradox.

The resolution of Denny's paradox, as described by Hu *et al.*, is that water striders transfer momentum not by surface ripples, but rather by vortices beneath the water surface. Unlike the circular vortices shed by fish, those created by water striders are squat affairs—a "U-shaped" filament with two free ends attached to the water surface. This peculiar shape is an elegant example of Helmholtz's laws, which govern the structure of vortex filaments. Vortex filaments cannot end abruptly within a fluid, and so must join end to end, as in a smoke ring, or attach to a wall or surface discontinuity, as in a tornado. By measuring the size and speed of the vortices formed behind the legs, the authors were able to show that the rearward momentum created was large enough to explain the insect's forward motion, whereas the contribution of the capillary waves was much too small. So, despite their small size, the legs of water striders are analogous to the oars of a rowing-boat, which also move forwards by sending a series of vortices backwards through the fluid. This more accurate understanding of water striders fits well with the emerging picture of animal locomotion. Through their use of vortices, water striders share general features with animals flying above and swimming below them.

References

1. Hu, D. L., Chan, B. & Bush, J. W. M. *Nature* **424**, 663–666 (2003).
2. Dickinson, M. H. *et al. Science* **288**, 100–106 (2000).
3. Kokshaysky, N. V. *Nature* **279**, 146–148 (1979).
4. Rayner, J. M. V. & Aldridge, H. D. J. *J. Exp. Biol.* **118**, 247–265 (1985).
5. Brodsky, A. K. *The Evolution of Insect Flight* (Oxford Univ. Press, 1994).

6. Lauder, G. V. & Drucker, E. *News Physiol. Sci.* **17**, 235–240 (2002).
7. Rayner, J. M. V. *J. Fluid Mech.* **91**, 697–730 (1979).
8. Ellington, C. P. *Phil. Trans. R. Soc. Lond. B* **305**, 115–144 (1984).
9. Denny, M. W. *Air and Water: The Biology and Physics of Life's Media* (Princeton Univ. Press, 1993).

How many young children have run up a ramp and leaped off it, hoping they could take off and fly? For children, these attempts are more likely to cause bruises than any sensation of soaring, but running up inclines could have been important in the evolution of birds from terrestrial to flying creatures. Kenneth Dial has found that chukar partridges—small birds related to chickens and turkeys—use their wings to help them run up steep slopes, even overhangs of up to 105 degrees. Birds usually use their wings to lift and propel themselves in the air. In the case of wing-assisted incline running, however, the chukars vary the angle of their wingbeats based on the steepness of the incline such that during nearly half of the wingbeat, the bird accelerates toward the surface. The force of this acceleration improves the bird's traction and allows it to run vertically. Friction is essential to this process—the birds were unable to scale smooth inclines angled at more than 60 degrees. Dial's research is causing researchers to reconsider the motion of other birds and their avian ancestors. —LEH

"Uphill Dash May Have Led to Flight"
by Elizabeth Pennisi
Science, January 17, 2003

A century-long flap among evolutionary biologists concerns how the ability to fly evolved in birds. Some propose that avian ancestors took wing by gliding from trees; others say early birds got a running start and lifted off the ground as they beat their feathered forelimbs. A new study suggests that neither idea is quite right.

Instead, flight may have evolved in protobirds that used their wings to scale inclined objects and trees, says Kenneth Dial, an experimental functional morphologist and behavioral ecologist at the University of Montana, Missoula. Dial's 15-year-old son clued him in to this new possibility. He claimed that he saw half-kilogram chukar partridges, whose flight development Dial studies, running straight up bales of hay. . . . Dial reports that the birds indeed flap their way up steep inclines—although not the way he and his colleagues would have thought—and suggests that avian ancestors may have done the same. Dial hypothesizes that in evolving the ability to climb ever steeper slopes, these animals came to move their forelimbs as modern birds do—up and down—instead of just back and forth like reptiles. This switch set the stage for flight, he explains.

His finding "has blown the field wide open," says Kevin Padian, an evolutionary biologist at the University of California, Berkeley. Chukars are related to chickens, quails, and turkeys. These galliform birds' flight and running dynamics might reflect those of their great, great ancestors—the birdlike dinosaurs. Like them, the modern descendants have wings but don't fly well, and their legs are strong.

Working with his son Terry and another high school student, Ross Randall, Dial monitored chukars' movements and found that newly hatched birds could walk up slopes of 45 degrees and could master steeper inclines by flapping their baby wings. They tackled ever steeper slopes as they matured. Even more remarkable, adults could sprint up overhangs of 105 degrees, sometimes climbing 5 meters. These skills declined when the researchers clipped or removed the birds' feathers.

Using high-speed video recordings and devices that monitor acceleration, Dial analyzed wing strokes and the effects of flapping on the bird's body. As the birds run up an incline, the films reveal, they flap their wings at a different angle than when they are flying. The net effect pushes the bird into the incline so that its feet don't slip—akin to spoilers on a race car. On a vertical surface, they hold their wings as if flying. "The films are amazing," says Padian. "[They] tell us something about living birds that we didn't know." Researchers interested in the evolution of bird flight are taking note, and some interpret the results as bolstering their own ideas. For those who think flight evolved from birds parachuting from trees, this behavior could solve the problem of how the birds got into the trees in the first place.

In contrast, Luis Chiappe, a paleontologist at the Natural History Museum of Los Angeles County, sees the findings as supporting his theory that flapping

wings led to ever faster running speeds that eventually made it possible to lift off. "Although [Dial's] view falls between the strict application of the ground-up and trees-down theories, I would place it closer to the realm of ground-up theories," he notes.

But Dial thinks his findings add a new scenario to the debate. "These animals are doing something that none have proposed," he says. The key innovation that allowed avian ancestors to fly, he claims, came as they evolved a new way of moving their forearms. Being able to flap wings up and down as well as back and forth was advantageous because it got the animals up steep surfaces. Once thus equipped, they could flap away as nature's first flyers, Dial says. It might be impossible to determine when this new ability developed, but analyses of some fossils indicate that protobirds—much like chukars—were able to flap their wings either back and forth or up and down.

Dial is now studying other, more primitive birds, such as South America's tinamous, to rule out the possibility that this locomotor skill evolved late in bird history. However, neither Dial nor his colleagues think the issue is settled. Indeed, Chiappe points out, "I imagine people will continue to argue about the origin of bird flight for a long time."

For thousands of years, humans have wondered about the Moon—how it was formed, what it is made of, and what its significance is. Now computer simulations of the early solar system and the movement of objects in it are providing insight into our satellite's origins.

Physics students are familiar with perfectly inelastic collisions, in which the two colliding objects become stuck together. Many researchers believe that a Mars-sized planet collided with a young Earth and stuck, but material from Earth was ejected during the collision and formed the Moon. The theory has problems, however, because of the Moon's orbit and angular velocity. Most models of giant impacts result in a moon orbiting much farther away than our satellite is today.

However, this article discusses models created by Robin Canup, Craig Agnor, and Harold Levison that suggest smaller impacts after the initial one could have tweaked the angular momentum of the Earth-Moon system. Is this

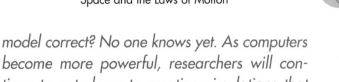

model correct? No one knows yet. As computers become more powerful, researchers will continue to get closer to creating simulations that accurately account for the data we have. —LEH

"Moon-Forming Crash Is Likely in New Model"
by Dana Mackenzie
Science, January 1, 1999

The greatest accident in Earth's history was probably no accident at all, according to new computer simulations of the early solar system. Planetary scientists believe that sometime in the first 100 million years after the solar system took shape from gas and dust, a Mars-sized planet smashed into Earth. The impact liquefied Earth's surface and ejected a huge blob of material that coalesced into the moon. Far from being a chance encounter that defied all the odds, the new simulations suggest, an impact like this is expected to occur in the solar system's first 100 million years.

"The lesson is that giant impacts are common," says Robin Canup of the Southwest Research Institute (SWRI) in Boulder, Colorado, who developed one of the models. "They're not the wild, ad hoc event that they were once believed to be." Her simulations, which were announced last month at the Origin of the Earth and Moon conference in Monterey, also tracked for the first time how smaller collisions following the giant impact could have tweaked Earth's rotation rate and the tilt of its axis to match what is seen today.

Don Davis and William Hartmann, now of the Planetary Science Institute in Tucson, Arizona, proposed the giant impact theory in 1975. By the mid-1980s, it had emerged as the leading explanation for the moon, largely because every other theory appeared to have fatal flaws. For example, "co-accretion," in which the Earth and moon grew up together, failed to explain why the moon has a much smaller iron core than Earth. The "fission" model, in which the moon spun off from the outer layers of Earth, failed to explain why the moon has an iron core at all. But planetary scientists embraced the impact scenario reluctantly, says Hartmann. "The big objection in those days was that a giant catastrophic collision seemed ad hoc to all the other workers."

Testing the idea by simulating the motion of the dozens of "protoplanets"—the building blocks of the planets—in the early solar system was impossible until recently. Computers weren't up to the task, and existing mathematical methods limited the length of time that could be modeled. After 100,000 orbits or so, the accumulated errors in the computations would cause the planets to fly away to infinity or spiral into the sun. Canup, Craig Agnor of the University of Colorado, Boulder, and Harold Levison of SWRI, however, use a new method called "symplectic integration," which prevents the energy of the virtual solar system from increasing, enabling researchers to model tens of millions of orbits.

Canup's simulations begin about 10 million years after the birth of the solar system, when gas and dust would have coalesced into about two dozen protoplanets, and continue until the full-fledged planets have settled into stable orbits, typically after about 100 million years. At this point, the inner solar system nearly always contains only four or five planets that have swept up all the rest. Usually, one or two of these planets have experienced impacts large enough to form a moon, Canup found. Two other research groups, relying on symplectic modeling techniques, have gotten similar results.

Planetary scientists agree that the new simulations are not the last word. "The problem with the simulations is that they are all primitive in one way or another," says Jack Lissauer of NASA's Ames Research Center in Mountain View, California, a member of one of the other modeling groups. In particular, all three models assume that colliding objects stick together like lumps of clay; in reality, many of the collisions probably threw out debris, affecting the size and orbit of the resulting body. (The new models don't actually show debris flying off to form the moon; they simply show impacts big enough to do the job.)

Still, Canup's simulation may resolve an inconsistency in the giant impact scenario: the difficulty of producing a collision large enough to get a moon-sized body into orbit, but with low enough angular momentum to produce the orbit seen today. Most plausible impacts would have resulted in a lunar orbit much farther out.

Earlier this year, Alastair Cameron of Harvard University proposed one solution. His model assumes the Earth was only two-thirds its present size when the impact occurred, allowing the impactor to be small and eliminating the angular momentum problem. If the collision took place early enough in planetary history, plenty of debris would have remained to feed the growth of Earth to its present size. But there's a snag: comparisons of the chemical compositions of the Earth and moon imply that the Earth was fully formed, or nearly so, when it spawned the moon.

Canup's simulations provide a different way out. They show that before or after the giant impact, Earth could have experienced a shower of small impacts, which could have slowed the rotation of the Earth-moon system. "Smaller impacts are very effective at tweaking the spin of a planet, even though they add very little mass," Canup says. Lissauer, however, is not convinced that Canup's solution escapes the problem of the similarity in Earth-moon composition, noting that his "back-of-the-envelope" calculation shows that the impactors would have added at least 4% of Earth's present mass after the moon had been born.

The new impact simulations also give astronomers who are searching other stars for planets like our own an extra tool. By making giant impacts a likelihood and smaller impacts a near certainty, the simulations suggest that the birth throes of moons like our own might be visible in other solar systems. Alan Stern of SWRI, who has calculated that a moon-forming impact should be detectable from a distance of 400 light-years, says the glow of such a cataclysm "would be the only way of detecting an Earth-sized planet in another solar system directly."

The early solar system in some ways resembled a pool table with balls rolling over it. However, when the ball-like protoplanets collided, they did not always bounce off each other. At certain velocities, they stuck to each other in perfectly inelastic collisions—a process called accretion. Planetesimals became planetary embryos, and eventually developed into Mercury, Venus, Earth, and Mars.

Motion was an important part of the planetary accretion process even beyond the actual collisions. For instance, each protoplanet exerted a gravitational pull on the protoplanets around it. This affected their orbits, which were often elliptical and crossed one another, and thus helped determine which protoplanets collided.

This article by Robin M. Canup looks at planetary accretion in general, and, more specifically, at the collision that formed the Moon. Researchers hope to eventually be able to view planet formation around other stars and thus confirm or discredit the various models and simulations that have been proposed. But for

*now, they must work with what makes sense
based on the laws of motion. —LEH*

"Origin of Terrestrial Planets and the Earth–Moon System"
by Robin M. Canup
Physics Today, April 2004

According to current theories, the overall architecture of our solar system was established more than 4 billion years ago through an era of planet formation lasting from 10 million to several hundred millions of years. Before we began learning about other planetary systems, it was natural to assume that our own was quite representative. But in the past decade, the discovery of about 100 planetary systems around other stars has challenged this view; these systems display a broad variation in structure and most do not closely resemble our own.[1]

Observational capabilities currently are limited to the detection of giant, Jupiter-sized planets around other stars, so that we are uncertain of the existence and distribution of smaller Earth-like planets in such systems. Thus planetary scientists rely on our own solar system as the case study for understanding the formation of terrestrial, solid planets and their satellites—such as Earth and the Moon. But our solar system as a whole may not be particularly characteristic, and recent observations suggest that the process of planet formation is one from which many potential outcomes may emerge. Theoretical models and computer simulations that strive to recreate the planetary formation process must therefore be able to account for both the primary characteristics of our system and the apparent diversity of extrasolar systems.

The Planetesimal Hypothesis

Understanding of stellar formation processes and observations of other young stars suggest that the early Solar System consisted of the newly formed Sun and an orbiting disk of gas and dust. If one assumes it had a roughly solar composition, such a disk—also referred to as the solar nebula—would contain a mass in hydrogen gas about 100 times that contained in solid particles. Isotopic dating of the oldest known meteorites indicates that macroscopic solids began to form within the gas-rich solar nebula about 4.56 billion years ago. Observations of other stellar systems suggest that the Sun's hydrogen-rich nebula would have been lost—possibly due to a strong solar wind or photoevaporation—after about 1–10 million years. At that time, the protoplanetary disk transitioned from one whose mass was predominantly gas to one composed solely of solid objects orbiting the Sun.

In this context, how did our solar system's large inner objects—Mercury, Venus, Earth, the Moon, and Mars—originate? The so-called planetesimal hypothesis, which in its modern form has been developed over the past 40 years, proposes that solid planets grow from initially small particles in the protoplanetary disk through collisional accumulation, or accretion. As solid objects orbit the Sun, mutual gravitational interactions and interactions with the gaseous nebula cause their elliptical orbits to cross, which leads to collisions. The

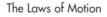
outcome of a given collision depends primarily on the ratio of the impact speed, v_{imp}^2, to the gravitational escape velocity of the colliding objects, v_{esc}, where $v_{esc} = \sqrt{2G(m_1 + m_2)/(R_1 + R_2)}$, G is Newton's gravitational constant, and m_1 and R_1 are the object masses and radii. The impact speed is a function of both v_{esc} and the relative velocity v_{rel} between the objects at large separation with $v_{imp}^2 = v_{esc}^2 + v_{rel}^2$, so that v_{imp} is always greater than or equal to v_{esc}.

For $v_{imp} \gg v_{esc}$, collisions result in rebound, erosion, or even fragmentation, while for lower-impact velocities, with $v_{imp} \sim v_{esc}$, energetically dissipative collisions lead to the formation of gravitationally bound aggregates. Repeated collisions with low impact velocities thus allow for the accretional growth of larger and larger objects.

Terrestrial planet accretion in our solar system is typically described in three stages: growth of approximately kilometer-sized "planetesimals" from dust and small particles; accretion of planetesimals into planetary embryos containing around 1–10 % of the Earth's mass $M_\oplus$; and the collision of tens to hundreds of planetary embryos to yield the final four terrestrial planets.

The processes that control growth during the first stage are the least well understood. In general, the interaction of small, subkilometer-sized particles with the nebular gas causes their mutual impact velocities to greatly exceed their gravitational escape velocities, so that growth during two-body collisions must instead rely on either non-gravitational surface sticking forces (such as van der Waals or electrostatic forces) between the colliding particles or the collective gravitational influence of neighboring particles. Such collective effects could become important if dynamical mechanisms exist that can concentrate solids in a region of the disk; in that case, an enhanced local spatial density of particles can allow groups of particles to collapse under their self-gravity to form larger objects. Whether kilometer-sized planetesimals were formed by sticking and binary collisions or by gravitational instability—or both—is a subject of active research.[2]

Planetesimals to Planetary Embryos

Once planetesimals become large enough (approximately kilometer-sized) for their dynamics and collisional growth to be controlled by gravitational interactions, a much better understanding exists of how growth proceeds. That understanding is due in large part to improvements in computational modeling techniques.

The rate of accretion is primarily controlled by the rate of collisions among orbiting planetesimals. Consider an annulus in the protoplanetary disk centered at some orbital radius a with volume $V = Ah$, where A is the mid-plane area and h is the disk thickness. If the annulus contains N small planetesimals with some characteristic random velocity v_{ran} relative to that of a circular orbit at radius a, then a larger embedded object of radius R will accumulate the small particles at an approximate rate

$$\text{Collision rate} \sim \frac{v_{ran} N(\pi R^2) F_g}{V} \approx n\Omega(\pi R^2)\left(1 + \frac{v_{esc}^2}{v_{ran}^2}\right), \quad (1)$$

where $F_g = 1 + (v_{esc}/v_{ran})^2$ is the gravitational enhancement to the collisional cross section due to two-body scattering, $n = N/A$ is the number of particles per surface area in the disk, and $h \approx v_{ran}/\Omega$, with Ω the Keplerian orbital angular velocity. Equation 1 has its roots in kinetic theory and is known as the "particle-in-a-box" collision rate. In the case of an orbiting "box" of planetesimals, the random particle velocities arise from the planetesimals' orbital eccentricities and inclinations and are analogous to the random thermal velocities of gas molecules confined to some volume. As this simple expression shows, the rate of collisions, and therefore of accretional growth, depends on the local Keplerian orbital velocity (which increases with decreasing distance from the Sun, so that regions closer to the Sun generally accrete more rapidly), the number density of planetesimals, and their sizes and relative velocities.

The mass and velocity distributions of a swarm of planetesimals are themselves dynamically coupled. Gravitational scattering among particles tends to increase v_{ran}, while energy dissipation during collisions and drag exerted on particles by the gaseous nebula both act to decrease v_{ran}. For a distribution of objects, an equilibrium between these processes yields v_{ran} on the order of the escape velocity of the object class that contains the majority of the total mass.

Interactions among orbiting particles of different masses tend to drive the system toward a state of equipartition of kinetic energy, with smaller particles having typically higher v_{ran} and the largest objects having the lowest. This effect is known as dynamical friction:

A swarm of background small particles acts to damp the velocities of the largest objects. From equation 1, if the largest objects in a given region of the disk also have the lowest velocities, then their collisional cross sections will be significantly enhanced, compared to those of smaller objects, due to the gravitational focusing factor, F_g. For large objects, v_{esc} will be large compared to v_{ran}, which will be controlled by the smaller planetesimals that still contain most of the system's mass. The largest objects thus grow the fastest, and a single object typically ends up "running away" with the great majority of the total available mass in its annular region in the disk. Through this so-called runaway growth, approximately lunar-sized objects, containing roughly 1 % of $M_\oplus$, grow in the inner Solar System in as little as 10^5 years.

Once a large object has consumed most of the mass in its annulus, growth slows, primarily due to the reduced amount of locally available material and planetesimal velocities that have increased to around v_{esc} of the largest embryo. Figure 2 shows the predicted distribution of planetesimal masses in a region extending between the current orbits of Mercury and Mars from a 10^6-year accretion simulation performed by Stuart Weidenschilling (of the Planetary Science Institute) and colleagues [see original article for figure].[3] After a million years, 22 large planetary embryos have formed in the inner Solar System and contain 90 % of the total mass. The embryos are radially well separated on nearly circular, coplanar orbits, with each containing a mass of at least 10^{26} g (for comparison, $M_\oplus \approx 6 \times 10^{27}$ g).

Late-Stage Terrestrial Accretion

Given our four terrestrial planets, the state shown in figure 2 with tens of "miniplanets" must have been a transitory one. The gaseous component of the solar nebula is expected to have dispersed after 10^6–10^7 years, and with it went an important source of velocity damping for small objects. As the random velocities of small objects increased, their ability to damp the velocities of the larger embryos through dynamical friction would decrease. Mutual gravitational interactions among the embryos would then become more potent and lead to the excitation of their orbital eccentricities, mutual orbit crossings, and finally embryo–embryo collisions and mergers. As the embryos collided and accreted, the number of planets would decrease and the dynamical stability of the system would increase, until finally a few planets on stable orbits remained. The final configuration of planets would thus be established in a stochastic "process of elimination," and a planet's dynamical characteristics—its mass, orbital radius, rotation rate and rotational axis, for example—would be greatly influenced by its last few large collisions.

Models of the accretion of planetary embryos into terrestrial planets were pioneered in the 1980s by George Wetherill (Carnegie Institution of Washington's Department of Terrestrial Magnetism), who utilized a Monte Carlo approach for tracking embryo orbits. Such statistical models use analytic approximations to estimate the likelihood of collisions and to describe the effects of mutual gravitational perturbations among the planetary embryos. Those techniques, however, could not incorporate some important dynamical effects, including the potential for successive and correlated close encounters between a given pair of embryos.

In the past decade, late-stage accretion models have been revolutionized by advances in methods for directly integrating the equations of motion of objects that orbit a more massive central primary. The key breakthrough was made in 1991 by Jack Wisdom (MIT) and Matthew Holman (now at the Harvard–Smithsonian Center for Astrophysics). The Wisdom–Holman mapping (WHM) method allows for accurate integrations with relatively long integration time steps.[4] Whereas classic orbit integrators require 500–600 time steps per orbit, WHM saves time by analytically tracking the Keplerian motion and integrating only the small perturbations that arise from the masses of the orbiting objects, so that only a few tens of time steps per orbit are needed to ensure accuracy. The WHM method is also symplectic: Although it does not exactly conserve energy, the predicted energy oscillates about a fixed value so that energy errors do not accumulate with time. Modern techniques[5] based on the WHM method can track the dynamical evolution of systems of several hundred accreting planetary embryos for more than 10^8 years.[6, 7] Such simulations follow not only the actual orbit of each embryo but also the dynamical encounters between embryos, including collisions or close passes.

Figure 3 shows the final planetary systems produced in eight late-stage accretion simulations recently performed using such direct integration techniques by

John Chambers of NASA's Ames Research Center [see original article for figure].[7] The simulated systems display a wide variety of architectures but are generally similar to our solar system's terrestrial planets in terms of the number of final planets and their masses. A notable difference is that the planets in the simulated systems have eccentricities and inclinations much higher than those of Earth and Venus, whose orbits are very close to circular and coplanar. This difference is likely a result of simplifications made in most of the models to date, namely ignoring the influence of potential coexisting small objects or a remnant of the gas nebula in the late stage. Both would generally act to decrease eccentricities and inclinations. While it is conceptually simplest to consider a sharp division between the middle and late stages so that in the late stage such effects can be ignored, Nature may not be so accommodating. Recent models that include more initial objects or a small portion of the nebular gas have found systems with orbits closer to those in our Solar System, although accounting for the nearly circular orbits of Earth and Venus remains an open issue.

A seemingly inherent feature of the late stage is giant impacts, in which lunar- to Mars-sized objects mutually collide to yield the final few terrestrial planets. Figure 4 shows the mass of impactors as a function of time for collisions that occurred in 10 late-stage simulations performed by Craig Agnor, Harold Levison, and me at the Southwest Research Institute [see original article for figure].[6] The "Earths" produced in those simulations require an average of 10–50 million years to accrete, with the largest late-stage impacts occurring predominantly in the 10^7- to 10^8-year time interval. The collisions display a random distribution of impact orientation, so that a final planet is as likely to end up rotating in the prograde sense (that is, in the same sense as its orbit about the Sun, as is the case for Mercury, Earth, and Mars) as in a retrograde sense (as is the case for Venus).

Origin of the Earth–Moon System

According to current thinking, the growing Earth experienced one such late-stage impact that ejected into orbit the material from which our Moon later formed. The giant impact theory for lunar origin is favored for its ability to account for the high angular momentum of the Earth–Moon system and for the iron-poor composition of the Moon. Reconciling the type of impact required with the actual Earth–Moon system thus provides an important benchmark for terrestrial-accretion models.

The impact theory proposes that the collision that created the Moon was also the primary source of the angular momentum $L_{\oplus\text{-}M}$ of the Earth–Moon system. The angular momentum delivered by an impactor of mass γM_T is

$$L_{\text{imp}} \approx 1.3 L_{\oplus\text{-}M} \, b \left(\frac{M_T}{M_\oplus}\right)^{5/3} \left(\frac{\gamma}{0.1}\right)\left(\frac{v_{\text{imp}}}{v_{\text{esc}}}\right) , \qquad (2)$$

where $b = \sin \xi$ is the impact parameter normalized to the sum of the impactor and target radii, ξ is the angle between the surface normal and the impact trajectory (so that a grazing impact has $b = 1$ and $\xi = 90°$), M_T is the total combined mass of the impactor and target,

and γ is the fraction of the total mass contained in the impactor. From this equation, a minimum impactor mass of about 0.08 $M_\oplus$, is required to yield $L_{\oplus-M}$ in the limit of a $b = 1$ grazing collision for $M_T \approx M_\oplus$, and $v_{imp} \approx v_{esc}$. Imparting the Earth–Moon angular momentum by an oblique impact with Earth thus implies an impactor roughly the size of Mars—that is, about 0.1 $M_\oplus$.

For impact-ejected material to achieve Earth-bound orbit, some modification to standard ballistic trajectories must occur, otherwise ejecta launched from the planet's surface either re-impacts or escapes. Two nonballistic effects are gravitational torques due to mutual inter-actions among ejected material or to interaction with a nonspherical distortion of the target planet, and pressure gradients associated with vaporization. These effects become important for large impacts: the first when the impactor is a significant fraction of the target's mass, and the second when the specific impact energy (that is, the impact energy per unit mass) exceeds the latent heat of vaporization for rock, about 10^{11} erg/g, which occurs for $v_{imp} \gtrsim 5$ km/s.

For a lunar-forming impact, the expected impact velocity is around 10 km/s, and both torques and vapor-ization could be important. Modeling potential lunar-forming impacts thus requires a full hydrodynamic approach that includes both an explicit treatment of self-gravity and an equation of state appropriate to describe the thermodynamic response of material subjected to very high impact energies and pressure.

Models of lunar-forming giant impacts have primarily used smooth particle hydrodynamics. SPH, developed over the past 25 years,[8] represents a significant advance in the modeling of deforming and spatially dispersing hydrodynamic systems, including giant impacts. SPH is a Lagrangian method, which is advantageous because its numerical resolution tracks the spatial distribution of the evolving material, and compositional histories can be easily followed. In SPH, a planetary object is represented by a great number of spherically symmetric overlapping "particles," each containing a quantity of mass of a given composition, whose three-dimensional spatial distribution is specified by a density-weighting function, the kernel, and by the characteristic width of the particle, the smoothing length.

For impacts between planet-scale objects, each particle's kinematic variables (position and velocity) and state variables (internal energy and density) evolve due to gravity, compressional heating and expansional cooling, and shock dissipation. The forces between particles thus include attraction due to gravity, which acts inversely with the squared distance between particles, and a repulsive pressure for adjacent particles closer than approximately the sum of their smoothing lengths. The equation of state relates a particle's specific internal energy and density to pressure as a function of input material constants.

The use of SPH in modeling lunar-forming impacts was pioneered by Willy Benz (now at the University of Bern), Alastair Cameron (now at the University of Arizona), and colleagues in the 1980s.[9] The general approach in performing such numerical impact experiments has been to vary the four impact variables—b, M_T, γ, and v_{imp}—of equation 2 in a series of simulations to determine what sets of impact conditions yield the most favorable results. The challenge is that the possible parameter space is large and individual impact simulations are computationally intensive. Recent works[10, 11] have successfully identified impacts capable of simultaneously accounting for the masses of Earth and the Moon, the Earth–Moon system angular momentum, and the lunar iron depletion.

Figure 5 shows a time series of a lunar-forming impact simulation[11] using high-resolution SPH and a sophisticated equation of state first developed at Sandia National Laboratories and recently improved by Jay Melosh of the University of Arizona's Lunar and Planetary Laboratory[12] to include a treatment of both molecular and monatomic vapor species [see original article for figure]. The simulation offers the most realistic treatment of vaporization of any SPH simulations performed to date, and each impact simulation requires several days of computational time on a high-speed workstation.

In the impact simulation, the colliding objects are described by a total of 60,000 SPH particles. The normalized impact parameter is $b \sim 0.7$ (that is, a 45° impact angle); the impactor contains 1.2 times the mass of Mars; the impact velocity is 9 km/s; and the impact angular momentum $L_{imp} = 1.25\ L_{\oplus-M}$. Before the impact, both objects are differentiated into iron cores and silicate mantles—a reasonable assumption given the amount of heating that would have been induced as the objects accreted to sizes this large. Both are 30% iron by mass.

After the initial oblique impact, a portion of the impactor is sheared off and continues forward ahead of the impact site. A distorted arm of impactor material extends to a distance of several Earth radii, and the proto-Earth surface and the inner portions of this arm rotate ahead of the more distant material. This configuration provides a positive torque to the outer portions of material, helping them to gain sufficient angular momentum to achieve bound orbit. In the 3- to 5-hour time frame, the inner portions of the orbiting material (composed primarily of the impactor's iron core) gravitationally contract into a semicoherent object that collides again with the planet after about 6 hours. Thus at this point, most of the impactor's iron has been removed from orbit. The outer clump of impactor material—composed entirely of mantle material—passes close to Earth and is sheared apart by planetary tidal forces that leave a circumplanetary disk after about a day.

At the end of this impact, the resulting planet and disk are a close analog to that needed to produce the Earth–Moon system. The planet contains about an Earth mass and its rotational day is about 4.6 hours, and the orbiting disk contains about 1.6 lunar masses. Of the orbiting material, approximately a lunar mass has sufficient angular momentum to orbit beyond a distance known as the Roche limit, located about 3 Earth radii from the center of the Earth for lunar-density material. Inside the Roche limit, planetary tidal forces inhibit accretion; it is within this distance, for example, that planetary ring systems are found around the outer planets. Accretion will occur for material orbiting beyond the Roche limit, so the orbiting disk produced by this impact would be expected to yield a lunar-sized moon at an initial orbital distance of about 3–5 Earth radii. The short 4.6-hour day of postimpact Earth causes the distance at which the orbital period is equal to the terrestrial day—the so-called synchronous radius—to fall within the Roche limit, at about 2.2 Earth radii. Because the Moon forms beyond this distance, tidal interaction with Earth will lead to the expansion of the Moon's orbit while Earth's rotation slows.

The impact must also account for the Moon's iron depletion. Whereas the colliding objects in figure 5 both contained 30 % iron by mass, the orbiting material is derived overwhelmingly from the outer mantle portions of the impactor. The protolunar disk contains only a few percent iron by mass, with the iron originating from the impactor's core. The lunar-forming impact dramatically raises Earth's temperature, with about 30 % of the planet's mass heated to temperatures in excess of 7000 K. Thus postimpact Earth would have been engulfed in a silicate vapor atmosphere, with the majority of the planet likely in a molten state.

Since large collisions appear typical in the late stages of terrestrial planet formation, how often do such impacts produce satellites? Results of impact simulations suggest that low-velocity, oblique collisions (those with $b > 0.5$) between planetary embryos generate some amount of orbiting material around the larger of the colliding objects. For random impact orientation, the most likely value for b is 0.7 (which is what has been found to be optimal for the Moon-forming impact), and 75 % of all collisions will have $b > 0.5$. Thus the inner Solar System may have initially contained many impact-generated satellites, with the majority lost as they were destroyed or dislodged by subsequent impacts or as their orbits contracted due to tidal interactions with a slow- or retrograde-rotating planet.

Isotopic Timing Constraints

The general agreement between the type of impact apparently required to yield Earth's Moon and those predicted by accretion simulations provides an important corroboration of current models of solid-planet formation. Other important pieces of independent evidence are the formation times implied by the isotopic compositions of Earth and the Moon.

A key development in the past decade has been the use of the hafnium–tungsten chronometer for dating planetary core formation and giant impacts.[13] Radioactive ^{182}Hf decays to ^{182}W with a halflife $\tau_{1/2}$ of 9 million years. A critical distinction between hafnium and tungsten is that hafnium is lithophilic ("silicate-liking," tending to be concentrated in oxygen-containing compounds such as silicates), whereas tungsten is siderophilic ("iron-liking," or tending to enter metallic phases). During core formation in a planetary object, whatever tungsten is present in the planet's mantle—radiogenic ^{182}W as well as nonradiogenic W-isotopes such as and ^{183}W and ^{184}W— will be largely removed from the mantle and incorporated into the iron core, while hafnium will remain in the mantle. Thus the mantle of a differentiated planetary object will have a Hf/W ratio larger than that of bulk

Solar-System composition. The bulk Solar-System composition can be inferred from the composition of primitive meteorites, called chondrites.

The Hf/W ratio and W-isotope compositions of a differentiated object such as Earth provide timing constraints on the formation of its core and potentially on the timing of its last large collision. The tungsten composition of chondrites includes both nonradiogenic isotopes and ^{182}W produced by the decay of primordial ^{182}Hf and the chondritic W-isotope composition provides a reference value believed indicative of early Solar System abundances. If a planet's core formed on a timescale shorter than about $5\tau_{1/2}$, its mantle, compared to chondrites, would contain excess ^{182}W (relative to the abundance of other W isotopes) produced by decay of ^{182}Hf after core formation. If the core formed later when ^{182}Hf was essentially extinct, all isotopes of W would have been equally depleted by incorporation into the iron core, leaving the mantle with a chondritic W-isotopic composition.

Earth's mantle contains an excess of ^{182}W compared to the most recent assessments of chondritic W-isotope composition,[14, 15] which implies that Earth's accretion and core formation were largely completed in 10–30 million years (see PHYSICS TODAY, January 2003, page 16). The Moon has a similar Hf-W–derived formation time of about 25–30 million years.[14] These specific timings can be affected by model assumptions, such as the degree to which accreting material isotopically equilibrates with Earth's mantle.[16] However, in general, the Hf–W timings and the late-stage dynamical models both yield estimates in the 10- to 50-million-year time interval for planetary accretion, giant impacts, and the final episodes of terrestrial-planet core formation. Broadly similar formation times of 10^7 to 10^8 years also result from other isotopic systems such as uranium–lead, iodine–xenon, and plutonium–xenon.[16] If the terrestrial planets had grown to their final sizes through runaway growth, their formation times would have been much shorter, on the order of 10^6 years or less. The agreement between the dynamically and geochemically derived timings thus provides significant support to the existence of a protracted phase of late accretion dominated by large impacts.

Whereas early models proposed that Earth-like planets form through the orderly accretion of nearby small material in the protoplanetary disk, current work instead suggests that solid planets are sculpted by a violent, stochastic final phase of giant impacts. The implication is that our terrestrial planets—and Moon—may only represent one possible outcome in a wide array of potential solar-system architectures. With future space missions (such as NASA's *Terrestrial Planet Finder*) devoted to detecting Earth-like planets around other stars, we may someday be able to directly test such concepts.

The author gratefully acknowledges support from NSF and NASA.

References

1. G. W. Marcy, P. R. Butler, *Annu. Rev. Astron. Astrophys.* **36**, 57 (1998); M. Mayor, *Annu. Rev. Astron. Astrophys.* (in press).

2. S. J. Weidenschilling, J. N. Cuzzi, in *Protostars and Planets III*, E. H. Levy, J. I. Lunine, eds., U. of Ariz. Press, Tucson (1993), p. 1031; W. R. Ward, in *Origin of the Earth and Moon*, R. M. Canup, K. Righter, eds., U. of Ariz. Press, Tucson (2000), P. 75; A. N. Youdin, E. I. Chiang, *Astrophys. J.* **601**, 1109 (2004).

3. S. J. Weidenschilling, D. Spaute, D. R. Davis, F. Marzari, K. Ohtsuki, *Icarus* **128**, 429 (1997).

4. J. Wisdom, M. Holman, *Astron. J.* **102**, 1528 (1991).

5. M. J. Duncan, H. F. Levison, M. H. Lee, *Astron. J.* **116**, 2067 (1998); J. E. Chambers, *Monthly Not. Royal Astron. Soc.* **304**, 793 (1999).

6. C. B. Agnor, R. M. Canup, H. F. Levison, *Icarus* **142**, 219 (1999).

7. J. E. Chambers, *Icarus* **152**, 205 (2001).

8. J. J. Monaghan, *Annu. Rev. Astron. Astrophys.* **30**, 543 (1992).

9. See, for example, the review by A. G. W. Cameron, in *Origin of the Earth and Moon*, R. M. Canup, K. Righter, eds., U. of Ariz. Press, Tucson (2000), p. 133.

10. R. M. Canup, E. Asphaug, *Nature* **412**, 708 (2001); R. M. Canup, *Annu. Rev. Astron. Astrophys.* (in press).

11. R. M. Canup, *Icarus* **168**, 433 (2004).

12. H. J. Melosh, *Lunar Planetary Sci. Conf.* **31**, 1903 (2000).

13. A. N. Halliday, D. C. Lee, S. B. Jacobsen, in *Origin of the Earth and Moon*, R. M. Canup, K. Righter, eds., U. of Ariz. Press, Tucson (2000), p. 45.

14. Q. Yin, S. B. Jacobsen, K. Yamashita, J. Blichert-Toft, P. Telouk, F. Albarede, *Nature* **418**, 949 (2002).

15. T. Kleine, C. Munker, K. Mezger, H. Palme, *Nature* **418**, 952 (2002).

16. A. N. Halliday, *Nature* **427**, 505 (2004).

17. W. K. Hartmann, R. J. Phillips, G. J. Taylor, eds., *Origin of the Moon*, Lunar and Planetary Institute, Houston, TX (1986).

18. R. M. Canap, K. Righter, eds., *Origin of the Earth and Moon*, U. of Ariz. Press, Tucson (2000).

Imagine that you are playing volleyball on a sand court. Someone misses the ball, and it bounces on the sand, leaving a depression. Interestingly enough, that depression is quite

similar to some of the craters on the Moon, though its order of magnitude is smaller.

Researchers are learning more about crater formation by simply dropping heavy round objects into granular materials, such as sand or sugar crystals. In many ways, these materials act more like liquids or gases than solids—the small particles flow over one another like molecules in a fluid. A solid ball would simply bounce off the surface of a block of metal or plastic, but in a collision with a granular material, the ball penetrates partway. It transfers momentum to some of the particles it hits, and these grains move in different ways depending on the precise conditions of the collision.

This article discusses research on energy, diameter, and depth in model collisions that create craters. The research provides more insight into the much larger craters that dot the Moon, Earth, and other planets. —LEH

"Craters in a Sandbox"
by Kim Krieger
Physical Review Focus, September 12, 2003

Large lunar craters have stories to tell about explosive collisions of meteorites with the moon. But to interpret them fully, researchers need to learn in detail how they are created. Two teams have discovered that balls dropped into sand and other granular matter form craters remarkably similar to those on the moon. In the

16 May *PRL*, one team reports the relationships between a colliding object's energy and the diameter and depth of impact craters. A second team, reporting in the 4 September *PRL*, recreated a variety of lunar crater shapes and examined the relationship between shape and energy of impact.

Some researchers have attempted to model meteorite impacts with explosive charges set in the ground, but the craters formed don't have the more complex features of large lunar craters. Still, geophysicists have developed a rule of thumb that both crater diameter and depth increase with impact energy according to a formula where energy is raised to the 1/4 power. Even so, says Douglas Durian of the University of California at Los Angeles (UCLA), the conventional theory doesn't give much insight into how the ground reacts to an impact, nor into what creates the distinctive crater shapes.

John de Bruyn, of Memorial University of Newfoundland in St. John's, Canada, says that his group wasn't originally interested in craters at all, but was considering the crown-shaped splash that appears when an object is dropped into a liquid. "We had just acquired a high-speed camera, and my post-doc was interested in seeing crown splashes in sand." It turned out that sand doesn't splash like a liquid, but the resulting pits looked a lot like craters on the moon.

De Bruyn's group dropped a steel ball into a container of glass beads of various sizes. They found that the geophysical rule of thumb for depth and diameter was approximately true, even though glass is nothing like moon rock, and the steel ball was hitting with much less energy than a meteorite. The team also showed that their crater structures were very similar to lunar craters. They created simple bowls with raised rims, bowls with small mountains in the middle, and bowls with rings around them, depending on the impact energy and bead size. The team now wants to learn in more detail how a variety of factors influence crater shape.

Durian and his colleagues dropped balls of many different materials and densities—from silicone rubber to ceramic—into materials such as sand, popcorn, and ice cream sprinkles. But the materials didn't matter much; the depth was mainly affected by the density and diameter of the ball and the height from which it was dropped. Their crater diameters followed the "energy to the 1/4 power" rule of thumb, but the depth didn't depend on energy in a simple way. This result doesn't contradict the work of de Bruyn's team because the UCLA researchers defined depth by measuring to the bottom of the buried ball, which was deeper than the bottom of the crater.

An old theory predicts a depth exponent of 1/4 by assuming that most of the meteorite's energy goes into lifting grains out of the crater space. But Durian suspects that granular materials can dissipate energy in a different way. At the early moments after impact, the grains may "seize up" and react like a solid mass before allowing the object to penetrate moments later. The same effect prevents you from slapping your open hand down through sand at the beach, even though it yields with a gentler push. Durian says that a better theory would account for this property and might agree more closely with his team's depth data.

"There is surely a great deal of internal energy dissipation that does not go into just lifting particles," says Robert Behringer of Duke University in Durham, North Carolina. He thinks Durian's paper is "potentially important." Lev Tsimring of the University of California at San Diego says that the two papers give him hope that researchers can "understand geological events by doing small-scale experiments and relatively simple simulations."

In the late 1800s, the engineer William Froude wanted to improve the design of British ships, which often contained flaws that caused them to sink. He built extremely accurate scale models of ships and tested them both in tanks and at sea. He found that a dimensionless variable, now called the Froude number, allowed him to compare the motions of the models to those of full-size ships.

The Froude number is now used in biology not only to compare the walking speeds of animals of different sizes, but also to determine how locomotion would be affected by different gravities. For example, films of astronauts on the Moon, where the gravity is only 16 percent of that on Earth, show the men moving very differently.

This article discusses research by G. A. Cavagna, P. A. Willems, and N. C. Heglund to determine the optimal walking speeds of a human *both at Mars's gravity (40 percent of Earth's) and at 150 percent of Earth's gravity. —LEH*

"Biomechanics: Walking on Other Planets"
by Alberto E. Minetti
Nature, January 25, 2001

A nineteenth-century equation used for building model ships allows us to compare the motion of animals of different sizes and gaits. It may also give us an idea of how we would move on different planets.

What do a gibbon swinging by its arms from tree to tree, a sailing steamship, and a walking human have in common? The answer lies in a simple concept introduced in the nineteenth century by nautical engineer William Froude to help him to produce model ships that maintained the same propulsion dynamics as full-size vessels. His "Froude number" is a dimensionless variable that was brought into biology by D'Arcy Thompson[1] and popularized by McNeill Alexander[2, 3] in the study of the energetics and mechanics of animal locomotion. This number allows one to compare the motion of species with different numbers of legs and gaits, and to investigate the effects of different body sizes on the mechanics of movement. As suggested by various earlier papers,[4–6] and borne out by new work described by Cavagna and colleagues in the *Journal of Physiology*,[7] the Froude number is also a reliable rule-of-thumb for predicting walking speeds on planets with gravities different from that of the Earth.

In walking humans or swinging gibbons, changes in the vertical position of the body's centre of mass during movement affect the gravitational potential energy of the body, and are accompanied by opposite changes in the kinetic energy needed to drive movement. The result is a pendulum-like mode of movement that saves mechanical energy. Roughly the same principles apply to ships, but here the potential energy is related to the size of the wave generated by the ship.

One of the theories underlying studies of movement—dynamic similarity[3]—basically states that geometrically similar bodies that rely on pendulum-like mechanics of movement will have similar gait dynamics if the Froude number remains the same. This number (Fr) is given by $Fr = v^2/(g \times l)$, where v is the speed of movement (in m s^{-1}), g is acceleration due to gravity (in m s^{-2}) and l is a characteristic length (such as leg length, in metres). The Froude number is directly proportional to the ratio between the kinetic energy and the gravitational potential energy needed during movement.

Dynamic similarity implies that, for example, despite differences in body size and number of legs, humans and quadrupeds change from walk to run or trot at the same Froude number, close to 0.5 (ref. 3). Even gibbons[8] change from merely swinging to swinging with aerial phases at Froude numbers ranging from 0.3 to 0.6. Humans of short height, such as children,[9, 10] patients suffering from early-onset growth-hormone deficiency[11] and pygmies,[12] optimally walk at speeds that correspond dynamically to that for adults, that is, with a Froude number of 0.25. Here, walking speed is optimal when the recovery of energy by the body—by exchanging potential and kinetic energies—is maximal.[7] What all of this means is that, within the same gravitational environment (such as on the Earth), the smaller the body, the lower the "equivalent" speed of movement, which is proportional to the square root of the leg length.

But the power of the Froude number for predicting equivalent walking speeds is not confined to the Earth. Within the same species and for a given body size, dynamic similarity also predicts that the lower the gravity, the slower the equivalent walking speed, which depends on the square root of the gravity ratio—the gravity of the planet in question divided by that of the Earth. On Earth, the optimal walking speed and walk-to-run-transition speed for an adult man of average height are, respectively, about 1.5 and 2.0 m s^{-1}. Figure 1 [see original article for figure] shows the relationships between walking speed and gravity at Froude numbers of 0.25 (which determines the optimal walking speed for humans) and 0.5 (which determines the walk-to-run-transition speed). One can use the Froude number to predict that the corresponding speeds on a stellar body with 16 % of the Earth's gravity, such as the Moon, will be about 40 % (the square root of 16 %) of those on Earth—that is, about 0.6 and 0.8 m s^{-1}, respectively.

These values were also predicted on the basis of a different approach about 35 years ago,[13] and the impossibility of walking at terrestrial speeds on the Moon has been clear to see in debriefings from the Apollo missions.[14] Moreover, experimental evidence has confirmed the predictive power of the Froude number in low gravity. Different low-gravity conditions have been simulated in the lab by applying a nearly constant upward force to the waist of subjects walking on a motorized treadmill.[4, 5] As predicted, the optimal walking speed[4] and the spontaneous transition between walking and running[5] occurred at Froude numbers close to 0.25 and 0.5, respectively. The slight discrepancy observed at low gravity is likely to be caused by the approximate nature of the simulation—limbs were allowed to swing normally, as if still affected by terrestrial gravity.

Cavagna *et al.*[7] now go further, to look at the mechanics of human walking in both low and high gravity. The low-gravity conditions correspond to those on Mars, being 40% of the Earth value. The high-gravity value was 150% of that on Earth. The authors used given portions of the parabolic trajectory of an aeroplane equipped with platforms that were sensitive to forces in all directions. In this way, Cavagna *et al.* measured the displacement of the body's centre of mass during a couple of walking steps at different constant gravities and walking speeds. From these measurements, they calculated the recovery of energy. They also recorded the speeds at which energy recovery was optimal (the optimal walking speeds). These speeds closely match those predicted when the Froude number is 0.25 (ref. 15), although the range of optimal speeds in high gravity is quite broad.

Indeed, Cavagna *et al.* conclude that increased gravity increases the range of walking speeds. This is again predicted by the Froude number . . . where the vertical distance between the curves increases with increasing gravity. Here, the vertical distance represents the range of speeds within two dynamically different conditions.

Bipedal and quadrupedal walking—unlike swinging—remain an approximation of ideal pendulum dynamics. Despite this, the Froude number, and the underlying theory of dynamic similarity, has so far proved a handy rule-of-thumb for predicting equivalent walking speeds as a function of body size or gravity. It is not yet known to what extent faster walking speeds can be maintained in high gravity for more than the few steps studied by Cavagna et al.[7] But it is nonetheless impressive that an idea introduced in the nineteenth century to produce model ships can be used in the twenty-first century to predict how humans would walk on other planets.

References

1. Thompson, D. W. On Growth and Form (Cambridge Univ. Press, 1961).
2. Alexander, R. M. Nature **261**, 129–130 (1976).
3. Alexander, R. M. Physiol. Rev. **69**, 1199–1227 (1989).
4. Griffin, T. M., Tolani, N. A. & Kram, R. J. Appl. Physiol. **86**, 383–390 (1999).
5. Kram, R., Domingo, A. & Ferris, D. J. Exp. Biol. **200**, 821–826 (1997).
6. Cavagna, G., Willems, P. A. & Heglund, N. C. Nature **393**, 636 (1998).
7. Cavagna, G., Willems, P. A. & Heglund, N. C. J. Physiol. (Lond.) **528**, 657–668 (2000).
8. Cheng, Y. H., Bertram J. E. & Lee, D. V. Am. J. Phys. Anthropol. **113**, 201–216 (2000).
9. Cavagna, G. P., Franzetti, P. & Fuchimoto, T. J. Physiol. (Lond.) **343**, 232–339 (1983).
10. Dejaeger, D., Willems, P. A. & Heglund, N. C. Pflügers Arch. Eur. J. Physiol. **441**, 538–543 (2001).
11. Minetti, A. E., Ardigò, L. P., Saibene, F., Ferrero, S. & Sartorio, A. Eur. J. Endocr. **142**, 35–41 (2000).
12. Minetti, A. E. et al. Eur. J. Appl. Physiol. **68**, 285–290 (1994).
13. Margaria, R. & Cavagna, G. Aerospace Med. **35**, 1140–1146 (1964).
14. Minetti, A. E. Proc. R. Soc. Lond. B **265**, 1227–1235 (1998).
15. Minetti, A. E. Acta Astron. (in the press).

5 Physics and Powerful Forces

Quantum mechanics has caused researchers to reevaluate many different concepts and ideas. For example, most physics students learn that a vacuum is a completely empty space, and for a long time, physicists believed that, too. However, quantum mechanics suggests that subatomic particles can suddenly exist where there was only empty space previously—and can wink back out of existence at any time. Because of this, a vacuum is not completely empty. An object at rest stays at rest until acted upon by a force, according to the laws of motion. The subatomic particles briefly existing in a vacuum can, however, cause an object to start to move in certain situations—to gain momentum when it previously had none.

This article discusses theoretical work by Alexander Feigel that suggests that this movement should be observable under particular conditions. Only careful experimental work will establish if he is correct, but empty space will never be quite so empty again. —LEH

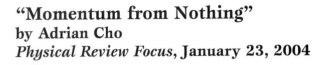

"Momentum from Nothing"
by Adrian Cho
Physical Review Focus, January 23, 2004

Nothing will come of nothing, avers Shakespeare's King Lear, but don't tell that to physicists. An object in strong electric and magnetic fields can siphon momentum out of the vacuum of empty space and begin to move, one researcher predicts in the 16 January *PRL*. The strange effect should be observable in the laboratory with current technologies.

The vacuum of empty space is a restless place. According to quantum mechanics, particles pop in and out of existence, and those "virtual" particles give the vacuum energy and can affect tiny objects. For example, two parallel metal plates will feel a minute force, called the Casimir effect, pulling them together. That's because virtual photons with certain wavelengths cannot exist between them. The vacuum outside the plates thus has more energy, so it squeezes the plates together.

But the vacuum can also possess momentum, says Alexander Feigel of Rockefeller University in New York, and it should be possible to transfer some of that momentum to a material object. To reach that conclusion, Feigel began by addressing a long-standing controversy in electrodynamics: How should one define the momentum of an electromagnetic field permeating matter? For nearly a century, physicists have had two definitions, one proposed by German physicist Max Abraham and another derived by German mathematician Hermann Minkowski. According to Abraham's formulation, the momentum of the electromagnetic field should be smaller in materials through which light travels more slowly; Minkowski's formulation states that in such materials the momentum should be bigger. Using relativity, Feigel found that the Abraham definition accounts for the momentum of the electric and magnetic fields alone, while the Minkowski definition also takes into account the momentum of the material.

Feigel next used his theoretical tools to analyze the momentum inside a material placed in strong, perpendicular electric and magnetic fields. He found that virtual photons traveling through the material would have a strange asymmetry. If the electric field pointed up and the magnetic field pointed north, then virtual photons of a given energy traveling east would have a different momentum from those traveling west. That asymmetry would give the vacuum a net momentum in one direction, and the material would have to gain momentum in the opposite direction to compensate. In fields of 100,000 volts per meter and 17 tesla—which can be created in the lab—the material should move at a rate of 50 nanometers per second, Feigel says, which should be measurable.

Others had reached similar conclusions about the meanings of the Abraham and Minkowski definitions of momentum, but Feigel's analysis is simpler, says Rodney Loudon of the University of Essex in Colchester, United Kingdom. "He's done it in quite a nice, elegant way," Loudon says. However, Ulf Leonhardt of the University of St. Andrews in Scotland says Feigel's approach may be a little too simple, as it treats the material as a macroscopic object and does not begin with the forces on the individual atoms in it. "There are definitely some subtleties that he's left out," Leonhardt says, though the results may still be correct.

Both Leonhardt and Loudon warn that the predicted effect may be difficult to spot. For example, Loudon says, if the material contains a few freely moving electrical charges, they will experience larger forces that may obscure the subtle quantum effect. Still, Leonhardt says, "This is a smart idea."

Science fiction writers may weave frightening tales based on the dangers of nanotechnology, but many scientists expect nanotechnology to revolutionize electronics, medicine, and other disciplines. Many devices have already become smaller over the past decade, and the shrinking continues.

One challenge for nanotechnology, however, is creating devices that will move in a directed fashion. Diffusion is the movement of particles from an area of high concentration to one of low concentration. Thermal agitation—movement resulting from heat—causes the particles to diffuse. When an object is very small, the thermal agitation can be much stronger than the inertial forces working on the object. In this case, the object cannot move in a directed fashion — it simply floats around at the mercy of diffusion.

This article looks at motion at the typical nanotechnology scale and different methods to overcome the diffusion problem. Corkscrews, flexible oars, ratchets, and other solutions will all likely be important in future nanodevices, although it is also probable that engineers will create something as yet undreamed of. —LEH

"Brownian Motors"
by R. Dean Astumian and Peter Hänggi
Physics Today, November 2002

A great challenge for the burgeoning field of nanotechnology is the design and construction of microscopic motors that can use input energy to drive directed motion in the face of inescapable thermal and other noise. Driving such motion is what protein motors— perfected over the course of millions of years by evolution—do in every cell in our bodies.[1]

To put the magnitude of the thermal noise in perspective, consider that the chemical power available to a typical molecular motor, which consumes around 100–1000 molecules of adenosine triphosphate (ATP) per second, is 10^{-16} to 10^{-17} W. In comparison, a molecular motor moving through water exchanges about 4×10^{-21} J (the thermal energy kT at room temperature) with its environment in a thermal relaxation time of order 10^{-13} s. Thus, a thermal noise power of about 10^{-8} W continually washes back and forth over the molecule. That power, which, according to the second law of thermodynamics cannot he harnessed to perform work, is 8–9 orders of magnitude greater than the power available to drive directed motion. For molecules, moving in a straight line would seem to be as difficult as walking in a hurricane is for us. Nonetheless, molecular motors are able to move, and with almost deterministic precision.

Inspired by the fascinating mechanism by which proteins move in the face of thermal noise, many physicists are working to understand molecular motors at a mesoscopic scale. An important insight from this work is that, in some cases, thermal noise can assist directed motion by providing a mechanism for overcoming energy barriers. In those cases, one speaks of "Brownian motors."[2] In this article, we focus on several examples that bring out some prominent underlying physical concepts that have emerged. But first we note that poets, too, have been fascinated by noise.

Bivalves, Bacteria, and Biomotors

Bacteria live in a world in which they are subject to viscous forces large enough that the inertial term $m\dot{v}$ in Newton's equation of motion can be safely ignored. The motion of the bacteria, governed by those viscous forces, is very different than the inertia-dominated motion that we know from everyday experience. Edward Purcell, in his classic article "Life at Low Reynolds Number," highlighted that difference by formulating what has come to be known as the scallop theorem.[3]

A scallop is a bivalve (a mollusk with a hinged shell) that could, in principle, move by slowly opening its shell and then rapidly closing it. (In fact, the scallop's method of locomotion is somewhat different.) During the rapid closing, the scallop would expel water and develop momentum, allowing it to glide along due to inertia. A typical scallop has a body length a of about a centimeter and propels itself at a speed v of several cm/s, that is, at several times its length per second. Thus, the Reynolds number, $R = av\rho/\eta$ (a dimensionless parameter that compares the effect of inertial and viscous forces), is about 100, where ρ is the density of the fluid (for water, the density is 1 g/cm^3) and η is the fluid's viscosity (for water, about 10^{-2} g/(cm·s)).

For organisms a few thousand times smaller than a scallop, also moving at several body lengths per second, the Reynolds number is much less than one. In that case, the glide distance is negligible. Because the motion generated by opening the shell cancels that produced on closing the shell, a tiny "scallop" cannot move. The mathematical reason is that motion at low Reynolds number is governed by the Navier–Stokes equation without the inertial terms, $-\nabla p + \eta\nabla^2 v = 0$. Because time does not enter explicitly into the equation, the trajectory depends only on the sequence of configurations, and not on how slowly or rapidly any part of the motion is executed. Hence, any sequence that retraces itself to complete a cycle—and that is the only type of sequence possible for a system such as a "scallop" with just one degree of freedom—results in no net motion.

With typical lengths of about 10^{-5} m and typical speeds of some 10^{-5} m/s, bacteria live in a regime in which the Reynolds number is quite low, about 10^{-4}.

Thus, bacteria must move by a different mechanism than that used by a "scallop." Our purpose is not to investigate how actual bacteria move (see the article "Motile Behavior of Bacteria" by Howard C. Berg in PHYSICS TODAY, January 2000, page 24) but to examine generic mechanisms by which locomotion at low Reynolds number is possible, with an ultimate focus on molecule-size Brownian motors.

Purcell described several locomotion mechanisms, all of which pertain to motion induced by cyclic shape changes in which, unlike the scallop's cycle, the sequence of configurations in one half of the cycle does not simply retrace the sequence of configurations in the other half. Here, we consider the two mechanisms shown in figure 1, the corkscrew and the flexible oar [see original article for figure].

The two mechanisms shown have different symmetries. The corkscrew mechanism avoids retracing its steps by its chirality. At low frequency, the bacterium moves a fixed distance for each complete rotation of the chiral screw about its axis. Thus, the velocity is proportional to the frequency. Reversing the sense of corkscrew rotation reverses the bacterium's motion. Slow enough rotation produces motion with essentially no dissipation, so we call the corkscrew an adiabatic mechanism.

On the other hand, the flexible oar relies on the internal relaxation of the oar curvature to escape the scallop theorem. At low frequency, the amplitude of the bending of the oar is proportional to the frequency and the velocity is thus proportional to the square of the frequency.

Because, in this case, relaxation and dissipation are essential, the flexible oar is an example of a nonadiabatic mechanism.[4]

The Role of Noise

The mechanisms in figure 1 illustrate how self propulsion at low Reynolds number is possible. A new problem arises, however, when particles have lengths characteristic of molecular dimensions, 10^{-8} or so.

In that case, diffusion caused by thermal noise (Brownian motion) competes with self-propelled motion. The time to move a body length a at a self-propulsion velocity v is a/v, while the time to diffuse that same distance is of the order a^2/D. Here, the diffusion coefficient D is given in terms of particle size, solution viscosity, and thermal energy by the Stokes–Einstein relation $D = kT/(6\pi\eta a)$. At room temperature, and in a medium whose viscosity is about that of water, a bacterium needs more time to diffuse a body length than it does to "swim" that distance. For smaller molecular-sized particles, however, a body length is covered much faster by diffusion. For molecular motors, unlike bacteria, the diffusive motion overwhelms the directed motion of swimming.

A solution widely adapted in biology is to have the motor on a track that constrains the motion to essentially one dimension along a periodic sequence of wells and barriers.[5] The energy barriers significantly restrict the diffusion. Thermal noise plays a prominent constructive role by providing a mechanism, thermal activation, by which motors can escape over the barriers.[6] (See also the article "Tuning in to Noise" by Adi R. Bulsara and Luca Gammaitoni in PHYSICS TODAY, March 1996, page 39.) The energy necessary for directed motion is provided by appropriately raising and lowering the barriers and wells, either via an external time-dependent modulation or by energy input from a nonequilibrium source such as a chemical reaction.

A Simple Brownian Motor

Figure 2 shows a simple example of a Brownian motor, in which a molecule-sized particle moves on an asymmetric sawtooth potential [see original article for figure]. Such an asymmetric profile is often called a ratchet after the beautiful example given by Richard Feynman in his *Lectures on Physics*, volume I, chapter 46 (Addison-Wesley, 1963). Feynman used his ratchet to show how structural anisotropy never leads to directed motion in an equilibrium system depicted in figure 2, the potential's cycling—which provides the energy input—combines with structural asymmetry and diffusion to allow directed motion of a particle, even against an opposing force. (An excellent simulation of the Brownian motor is at the Web site http://monet.physik.unibas.ch/~elmer/bm/.)

For biological motors on a track, one might expect the length a and track period L to be of molecular size and the viscous drag coefficient to be around 10^{-10} kg/s, somewhat higher than that in water due to friction between the motor and track. If the potential is switched on and off with a frequency of 10^3 Hz, consistent with the rate of ATP hydrolysis by many biological motors, the induced velocity is about 10^{-6} m/s and the force necessary to stop the motion is approximately 10^{-11} N. The velocity and force estimates are both consistent with values obtained from single-molecule experiments on biological motors.[1] (See also the article "The Manipulation of Single Biomolecules" by Terence Strick, Jean-François Allemand, Vincent Croquette, and David Bensimon in PHYSICS TODAY, October 2001, page 46).

An effect analogous to the directed motion caused by cyclically turning a potential on and off can be demonstrated for particles moving on a fixed asymmetric track such as a sawtooth etched on a brass slide.[7] The energy input driving the directed motion is provided by cyclically varying the temperature between high and low values. At high temperatures the particles diffuse, but when the temperature is low the particles are pinned in the potential wells. Because of the asymmetry of the track, the fluctuations over time between hot and cold cause the particles to move, on average, over the steeply sloped, shorter face of the etched sawtooth.

In the scheme depicted in figure 2, the fuel is the energy supplied by turning the potential on and off. The track, or substrate, is the lattice on which the particle moves. The particle is the motor—the element that consumes fuel and undergoes directional translation. The model illustrates the two main ingredients necessary for self-propelled motion at low Reynolds number: symmetry breaking and energy output. The particle in the illustrated scheme is a true Brownian motor, because without thermal noise to cause Brownian motion, the mechanism fails.[8]

The ratchet in figure 2 mimics a Brownian motor first proposed in 1992 by Armand Ajdari and Jacques Prost working at the Ecole Supérieure de Physique et de Chimie Industrielles in Paris.[9] They envisioned a situation in which turning on and off an asymmetric electric potential would provide a means for separating particles based on diffusion.

Several groups explored that possibility in various ways during the mid-to-late 1990s.[10] In 1994, Ajdari and Prost, along with colleagues Julienne Rousselet and Laurence Salome, constructed a device for moving small latex beads unidirectionally in a non-homogeneous electric potential that was turned on and off cyclically. About 1 year later, Albert Libchaber and colleagues at Princeton University and at NEC Research Institute Inc, made an optical ratchet. By modulating the height of the barrier on an asymmetric sawtooth fashioned from light, they could drive a single latex bead around in a circle. Most recently, Joel Bader and colleagues at CuraGen Corp constructed a device for efficient separation of DNA molecules using interlocking combed electrodes with an asymmetric spacing between the positive and negative electrodes.

General Description

When we considered the scallop theorem and the devices bacteria use to evade it, we focused on physical changes—the opening and closing of a scallop's shell, the turning of a corkscrew, and the waving of a flexible flagellum. In a general mathematical description of motion at low Reynolds number, a time-dependent potential corresponds to the changes in shape that we discussed earlier.

Imagine a particle constrained to move on a line, with a spatially periodic time-modulated potential $V(x, t)$. The particle is governed by the equation of motion

$$m\dot{\upsilon} + V'(x, t) = -\gamma\upsilon + \sqrt{(2kT\gamma)}\xi(t) \ .$$

where the prime denotes a spatial derivative and $\gamma = 6\pi\eta a$ is the viscous drag coefficient. The left-hand side of the equation of motion describes the deterministic, conservative part of the dynamics, and the right-hand side accounts for the effects of the thermal environment— viscous damping and a fluctuating force modeled by thermal noise $\xi(t)$. If both inertia and noise are negligible, the equation of motion may be approximated as $V'(x, t) = -\gamma\upsilon$. Explicit time dependence enters only through $V'(x, t)$. Thus, the pattern of motion is independent of whether the modulations occur rapidly or slowly. If, as is the case for a standing-wave modulation, the changes are such that the path in the second half of the cycle retraces those of the first, then the velocity must also retrace its steps. That retracing is irrespective of the amplitude, waveform, or frequency of the modulation.

For Brownian motors, however, there is ineluctable and significant thermal noise, which changes the situation dramatically. Because noise provides a mechanism for relaxation—an internal response of the system to a change in the external parameters—a single external degree freedom can combine with the internal dynamics to escape the scallop theorem and yield directed motion, as in the scheme depicted in figure 2. In boxes 2 and 3, we have worked out a second illustrative scheme in detail and discussed the relationship of that scheme with the principle of detailed balance [see original article for boxes].

As illustrated in the first of those boxes, the net current (an appropriately normalized average velocity) due to modulation of the potential can be broken into two contributions. One is a purely geometric term corresponding to motion similar to that induced by a slow traveling–wave modulation. That term depends only on the two external parameters that define the modulation and describes the reversible part of the transport. Similar in spirit to the Berry, or geometric, phase in quantum mechanics (see the article "Anticipations of the Geometric Phase" by Michael Berry in PHYSICS TODAY, December 1990, page 34), that first term corresponds to the adiabatic transport mechanism described by David Thouless and recently used by Charles Marcus and his colleagues to pump electrons through a quantum dot with essentially no energy dissipation (see PHYSICS TODAY, June 1999, page 19).[11]

The second term corresponds to the dissipative part of the transport and is the term typically associated with the ratchet effect: In the on–off ratchet shown in figure 2, the average of the adiabatic term is zero—all of the net transport is described by the irreversible term. The dissipative nature of the mechanism corresponding to the irreversible term means that even random fluctuations such as those that might arise from a simple two-state nonequilibrium chemical reaction can drive transport.[12]

Two-Dimensional Ratchets

The Brownian motors we have considered so far have been confined to one spatial dimension and subject to time-varying potentials. One can develop a sharper intuition for Brownian ratchets by mapping time-modulated potentials into static, 2D potentials: $(x/L, \omega t) \rightarrow (x/L_x, y/L_y)$. The modulation, instead of being characterized by functions of time, is then characterized by functions of the coordinate y.[13, 14] The nonequilibrium features implicit in the original external temporal modulation are introduced by external forces in the x or y directions.

The resulting 2D potentials yield two classes of devices distinguished by symmetry. In one class, proposed by Tom Duke and Bob Austin, symmetry is broken in both coordinates in the sense that changing the sign of either x or y changes the potential. A member of this symmetry class is illustrated in figure 3a, which also shows the response of particles to forces in the up and down directions [see original article for figure]. Note that changing the direction of the force changes the direction of the resulting velocity. In general, for potentials with broken symmetry in both coordinates, to leading order, the x-component of current resulting from a force in the y direction is the same as the y-component of current resulting from the same magnitude force in the x direction. Generally, if the force in the, say, x direction is zero, current in both the x and y directions is proportional to the force in the y direction.

In the second class of devices, suggested by Imre Derényi and Dean Astumian and by Axel Lorke and colleagues, symmetry is broken in only one coordinate. Figure 3b shows a member of this class, with broken symmetry in the x coordinate [see original article for figure]. The figure also shows that a force up or down induces flow to the right; by symmetry, a force in the x direction induces no net flow in the y direction. An algebraic manifestation of those responses to force is that, to lowest order, the particle current in the x direction is proportional to the square of the y component of force.

An advantage of the second class is that an oscillating force in the y direction can drive unidirectional motion in the x direction, thus allowing devices to be much smaller. One can achieve good lateral separation without particles traveling very far vertically. Combining systems with different symmetry properties may make it possible to tailor a potential for the most effective separation in a given system.

So far, only the first symmetry class has been applied experimentally for particle separation,[13] but the second has been realized for ratcheting electrons that move ballistically through a maze of antidots.[14] Electrons in a 2D square array of triangular antidots move in a potential similar to that shown in figure 3b. When irradiated by far-infrared light, the electrons are shaken and crash against the antidots rather like balls hitting the obstacles on a pinball table. The electrons are then funneled into the narrow gaps between the antidots, thereby yielding a well-directed beam. Indeed, one observes a net photovoltage between source and drain—merely the expected ratchet effect that turns an AC source into a DC one.

Two-dimensional ratchets open a doorway to wireless electronics on the nanoscale. For example, different orientations of asymmetric block structures may allow for the guiding of several electron beams across each other. As suggested by Franco Nori and his collaborators at the University of Michigan, specially tailored 2D potentials, combined with a source of thermal or quantum noise, can provide a lens for focusing or defocusing electrons, much as optical lenses manipulate light.[15]

Ratchets in the Quantum World

Symmetry breaking and the use of noise to allow randomly input energy to drive directed motion can also be exploited when quantum effects play a prominent role. An especially appealing possible application is the pumping and shuttling of quantum objects such as electrons along previously selected pathways without the explicit use of directed wire networks or the like.

One of the most important features of quantum transport not present in the classical regime is quantum tunneling. Tunneling provides a second mechanism—the first being the thermal activation exploited for classical ratchets—for a particle to move among energy wells. Heiner Linke and colleagues took brilliant advantage of the two mechanisms in designing a quantum ratchet showing a current reversal as a function of temperature (see figure 4)[16] [see original article for figure]. Peter Hänggi and coworkers applied quantum dissipation theory to a slowly rocked ratchet device to theoretically anticipate such a current reversal.[17]

Using electron beam lithography, Linke and coworkers constructed an asymmetric electron waveguide within a 2D sheet of electrons parallel to the surface of an aluminum-doped gallium arsenide/gallium aluminum arsenide heterostructure. The device comprised a string of funnel-shaped constrictions, each of which forms an asymmetric energy barrier for electrons traveling along the waveguide. A slow (192 Hz), zero-average, periodic, square-wave voltage was applied along the channel to rock the ratchet potential. In other words, electrons traveling through the waveguide were subjected to a uniform perturbing force that periodically switched direction.

At low temperature, tunneling predominates. The barriers are narrowed when the force is to the right and widened when the force is to the left, thus inducing electron current to the right. Because of the asymmetry, the rocking produces a net current. At high temperatures, where thermal activation predominates, electrons move preferentially over the gentle slope of the potential. That movement leads to an electron current to the left. Moreover, the device functions as a heat pump even when the temperature is set to the value that produces no net electrical current: The thermally activated current is predominantly due to electrons in higher-energy states whereas the tunneling current is mainly due to electrons in the lower-energy states.[17]

Quantum ratchets are potentially useful in any number of tools such as novel rectifiers, pumps, molecular switches, and transistors. Some day, devices built with quantum ratchets may find their way into practical applications.

Perspective and Overview

A Brownian motor is remarkably simple: The essential structure consists of two reservoirs, A and B, with two pathways between them. (In the example of box 2, the two pathways are defined by whether the potential barrier overcome is to the left or right of well A.) By periodically or stochastically altering both the relative energies of the reservoirs and the "conductances" of the pathways between them, with a fixed relationship between the two modulations, one can arrange that transport from A to B is predominately via one pathway and transport from B to A is via the other pathway. Depending on the topology, the induced particle motion could be realized as directed transport along a circle or a line, transfer of microscopic cargo or electrons between two reservoirs, or coupled transport in two dimensions.

In micro- and nanoscale materials such as polymers or mesoscopic conductors, thermal activation and quantum mechanical tunneling are mechanisms for overcoming energy barriers (incidentally introducing nonlinearity).[6] In addition, the multiple time scales inherent in complex systems allow the necessary correlations between the fluctuations of the conductances and energies to emerge spontaneously from the dynamics of the system. In those cases, noise plays an essential or even dominating role: It cannot be switched off easily and, moreover, in many situations, not even the direction of noise-induced transport is obvious! Because the direction and speed of transport depend on different externally controllable parameters—temperature, pressure, light, and the phase, frequency, and amplitude of the external modulation—as well as on the characteristics of the potential and on the internal degrees of freedom of the motor itself, synthetic Brownian molecular motors can be remarkably versatile.[18]

In the microscopic world, "There must be no cessation / Of motion, or of the noise of motion" (box 1). Rather than fighting it, Brownian motors take advantage of the ceaseless noise to move particles efficiently and reliably.

R.D.A. thanks Anita Goel for many stimulating discussions and Ray Goldstein for an inspiring series of lectures on biopolymers. We thank our colleagues for their help and comments, particularly Howard Berg, Hans von Baeyer, Imre Derényi, Igor Goychuk, Dudley Herschbach, Gert-Ludwig Ingold, Heiner Linke, Manuel Morillo, Peter Reimann, Peter Talkner, and Tian Tsong.

References

1. S. M. Block, *Trends Cell Biol.* **5**, 169 (1995); J. Howard, *Nature* 389, 561 (1997); R. D. Vale, R. D. Milligan, *Science* **288**, 88 (2000).
2. P. Hänggi, R. Bartussek, in *Nonlinear Physics of Complex Systems: Current Status and Future Trends* (Lecture Notes in Physics, vol. 476), J. Parisi, S. C. Müller, W. Zimmerman, eds., Springer-Verlag, New York, (1996), 294; F. Jülicher, A. Ajdari, J. Prost, *Rev. Mod. Phys.* **69**, 1269 (1997); H. D. Astumian, *Science* **276**, 917 (1997). A comprehensive review is given by P. Reimann, *Phys. Rep.* **361**, 57 (2002). See also the articles in the special issue on "Ratchets and Brownian Motors: Basics, Experiments, and Applications," *Appl. Phys. A* **75** (August 2002).
3. E. Purcell, *Am. J. Phys.* **45**, 3 (1977).
4. R. D. Astumian, I. Derényi, *Phys. Rev. Lett.* **86**, 3859 (2001); M. G. Vavilov, V. Ambegaokar, I. L. Aleiner, *Phys. Rev. B* **63**, 195313 (2001).
5. P. H. von Hippel, O. G. Berg, *J. Biol. Chem.* **264**, 675 (1989).
6. P. Hänggi, P. Talkner, M. Borkovec, *Rev. Mod. Phys.* **62**, 251 (1990).
7. P. Reimann, R. Bartussek, R. Häussler, P. Hänggi, *Phys. Lett. A* **215**, 26 (1996).

8. M. O. Magnasco, *Phys. Rev. Lett.* **71**, 1477 (1993); R. D. Astumian, M. Bier, *Phys. Rev. Lett.* **72**, 1766 (1994); H. Bartussek, P. Hänggi, J. G. Kissner, *Europhys. Lett.* **28**, 459 (1994); J. Prost, J.-F. Chauwin, L. Peliti, A. Ajdari, *Phys. Rev. Lett.* **72**, 2652 (1994); C. R. Doering, W. Horsthemke, J. Riordan, *Phys. Rev. Lett.* **72**, 2984 (1994).

9. A. Ajdari, J. Prost, *C. R. Acad. Sci., Paris* **t. 315** (series no. 2), 1635 (1992).

10. J. Rousselet, L. Salome, A. Ajdari, J. Prost, *Nature* **370**, 446 (1994); L. Faucheaux, L. S. Bourdieu, P. D. Kaplan, A. J. Libchaber, *Phys. Rev. Lett.* **74**, 1504 (1995); J. S. Bader et al., *Proc. Natl. Acad. Sci. USA* **96**, 13165 (1999).

11. D. J. Thouless, *Phys. Rev. B* **27,** 6083 (1983); P. W. Brouwer, *Phys. Rev. B* **58**, R10135 (1998); M. Switkes, C. M. Marcus, K. Campman, A. C. Gossard, *Science* **283**, 1905 (1999); M. Wagner, F. Sols, *Phys. Rev. Lett.* **83**, 4377 (1999).

12. T. Y. Tsong, R. D. Astumian, *Bioelectrochem. Bioenerg.* **15**, 457 (1986); R. D. Astumian, P. B. Chock, T. Y Tsong, H. V. Westerhoff, *Phys. Rev. A* **39**, 6416 (1989).

13. T. A. J. Duke, R. H. Austin, *Phys. Rev. Lett.* **80**, 1552 (1998); G. W. Slater, H. L. Guo, G. I. Nixon, *Phys. Rev. Lett.* **78**, 1170 (1997); I. Derényi, R. D. Astumian, *Phys. Rev. E.* **58** 7781 (1998); D. Ertas, *Phys. Rev. Lett.* **80**, 1548 (1998); A. van Ouderaarden et al., *Science* **285**, 1046 (1999); C. Keller, F. Marquardt, C. Bruder, *Phys. Rev. E.* **65**, 041927 (2002).

14. A. Lorke et al., *Physica B* **249**, 312 (1998).

15. J. F. Wambaugh et al., *Phys. Rev. Lett.* **83**, 5106 (1999); C. S. Lee, B. Jankó, I. Derényi, A. L. Barabasi, *Nature* **400**, 337 (1999).

16. H. Linke et al., *Science* **286**, 2314 (1999).

17. P. Reimann, M. Grifoni, P. Hänggi, *Phys. Rev. Lett.* **79**, 10 (1997). I. Goychuk, P. Hänggi, *Europhys. Lett.* **43**, 503 (1998).

18. T. R. Kelly, H. De Silva, R. A. Silva, *Nature* **401**, 150 (1999); N. Koumura et al., *Nature* **401**, 152 (1999); Z. Siwy, A. Fulinski, *Phys Rev Lett.* **89**, 158101 (2002); J. Vacek, J. Michl, *Proc. Natl. Acad. Sci. USA* **98**, 5481 (2001).

Reprinted with permission from "Brownian Motors," by Astumian, R. Dean, and Peter Hänggi, *Physics Today*, pp. 33–39, November 2002. © 2002 American Institute of Physics.

News coverage of earthquakes generally focuses on the fallen buildings and lives lost when the ground begins to shake violently. But physicists focus on the forces and motions involved in

earthquakes. Their work could eventually lead to more reliable methods to predict "the big one."

The earth's crust is not continuous; it is made of large pieces called tectonic plates. Most earthquakes happen at faults—places where these plates come together. Shear stress—force per unit area applied tangent to a plane—builds up beneath the surface. When this shear stress becomes greater than the frictional stress keeping the plates still, the plates move suddenly. The earthquake stops when the frictional stress becomes greater than the shear stress again.

This article by Hiroo Kanamori and Emily E. Brodsky looks at the physics of earthquakes in more detail, including spring systems that researchers use as models of faults, and a discussion of how lubrication of the rocks can affect the energy radiated by a quake. Researchers still have a lot to learn about earthquakes, but the basic concepts of force, friction, and energy are keys to a greater understanding of their mysterious and awe-inspiring processes. —LEH

"The Physics of Earthquakes"
by Hiroo Kanamori and Emily E. Brodsky
Physics Today, June 2001

Seismologists have never directly observed rupture in Earth's interior. Instead, they glean information from seismic waves, geodetic measurements, and numerical experiments.

The recent earthquakes in Taiwan, Turkey, and India tragically demonstrate the abruptness with which earthquakes occur and the devastation that often accompanies them. Scientists, emergency officials, and the public are greatly interested in earthquakes—sudden fractures in Earth's crust followed by ground shaking—and have many questions about them. For example, When do earthquakes occur? More precisely, what long-term processes and short-term triggers produce earthquakes? Although plate tectonics has provided a successful framework for understanding the long-term processes, the short-term triggers remain obscure, making earthquakes unpredictable. An equally important question and a fundamental challenge to the science of geophysics is, What happens during an earthquake? That is, What are the forces and motions during a seismic event? The answer to this question has practical consequences for mitigating the effects of the expected ground motion.

One of the most challenging aspects of studying earthquakes is obtaining observational constraints. Most earthquakes occur at depths down to 50 km, but some as deep as 670 km have been observed in certain regions. Seismologists have never directly observed ruptures occurring in Earth's interior. Instead, they rely on the information gleaned from the few available types of data, the most important of which is the record of seismic waves. During an earthquake, sudden crustal motion excites elastic waves that travel through Earth and are observable at seismic stations on the surface. These waves carry information about the movements at the earthquake's source, but the complex structure of Earth between the source and the receiver often complicates extracting the information from the signal. Despite this difficulty, researchers have learned much from seismic records and can determine the detailed rupture history of many recent seismic events.

Geological observations of exhumed faults (old faults formed at depths of about 5–10 km and brought to the surface by long-term uplift), geodetic measurements of crustal motion, heat-flow measurements, and laboratory-analog experiments have all significantly added to our information base. Even a simple catalog of when and where earthquakes occur helps to identify patterns that may point to common causes or to interactions between events (see PHYSICS TODAY, April 2000, page 59).

Earthquake physicists attempt to link the available observations to the processes occurring in Earth's deep interior to help them interpret the types of data just described. A few approaches or paradigms are commonly used to create these links. For example, plate tectonics links geodetic observations to the stresses that generate earthquakes over geological time scales. Models of frictional behavior link laboratory-analog and certain seismic waveform features to the stress changes occurring during an earthquake. In this review, we cover a few of the most commonly used approaches in earthquake physics.[1] Some more recent and speculative ideas provide an insight into possibly fertile future directions of research. Throughout, we are driven by the question, What happens during an earthquake?

Long-Term Processes

The forces generated in Earth's crust are typically described in terms of the shear stress and the shear strain. The shear stress is the force per unit area applied tangent to a plane. The shear strain is a dimensionless quantity that describes the distortion of a body in response to a shear stress . . . In this article we are concerned with shear forces and their effects, so for brevity, we do not use "shear" when discussing stresses and strains.

Long-term loading has traditionally been measured by geodetic and geological methods. Recent progress in space-based geodesy, made possible by the global positioning system and satellite interferometry, now provide us with a clear pattern of crustal movement and strain accumulation. Figure 1 shows recent geodetic measurements in California [see original article for figure]. The relative plate motion determined from these data is about 2–7 cm/year, which translates into a strain accumulation rate of approximately 3×10^{-7}/y along plate boundaries. The strain also accumulates in plate interiors, but at a much slower rate of about 3×10^{-8}/y or less. Since the rigidity of the crustal rocks is about 3×10^{4} MPa, this corresponds to a stress accumulation rate of 10^{-2} MPa/y along plate boundaries, an order of magnitude less in plate interiors.

When the stress at a point in the crust exceeds a critical value, called the local strength, a sudden failure occurs. The plane along which failure occurs is called the fault plane and the point where failure initiates is called the focus. Typically, there is a sudden displacement of the crust at the fault plane following the failure, and elastic waves are radiated. This is an earthquake. For most earthquakes, the displacement occurs at an existing geological fault, that is, a plane that is already weak.

The strain change, or coseismic strain drop, associated with large earthquakes has been estimated using geodetic and seismological methods. It ranges roughly from 3×10^{-5} to 3×10^{-4}, as demonstrated by Chuji Tsuboi's pioneering analysis of the 1927 Tango, Japan, earthquake.[2] The corresponding change in stress, called the static stress drop, is about 1–10 MPa, which is at least an order of magnitude smaller than the several hundred MPa needed to break intact rocks in the laboratory.

Dividing the coseismic strain drop by the strain accumulation rate suggests that the repeat times of major earthquakes at a given location are about 100–1000 years on plate boundaries, and about 1000–10,000 years within plates. These values agree with what has been observed at many plate boundaries and interiors.

Figure 2a schematically shows the development over time of stresses that generate earthquakes [see original article for figure]. Although the basic process is well understood and accurately measured, its details are quite complex. For example, the stress accumulation rate is not uniform over time. A large earthquake on a segment of a fault changes the stress on the adjacent segments, either statically or dynamically, and accelerates or decelerates seismic activity, depending on the fault geometry. The strength of the crust is not constant over time either. Migrating fluids may weaken Earth's crust significantly, altering the times at which earthquakes occur. The stress drop during earthquakes may also vary from event to event. These complicating factors and their effect on the intervals between earthquakes are illustrated in figure 2b [see original article for figure]. The overall long-term process is regular, but considerable temporal fluctuations of seismicity occur, making accurate prediction of earthquakes extremely difficult.

Short-Term Processes and Friction

Earthquake fault motion can be viewed as frictional sliding on a fault plane. The friction changes as a function of slip (relative displacement of the two sides of the fault plane), velocity, and history of contact. Thus, frictional stress controls seismic motion. An earthquake can occur only if friction decreases rapidly with slip, a process referred to as slip weakening. If friction increases with slip, or does not drop rapidly enough, slip motion either stops or occurs gradually. We treat only the slip-weakening case in this article . . .

In general, fault motion does not occur smoothly, but rather in a stop-and-go fashion, called stick-slip. The dynamic effects leading to stick-slip behavior have been studied extensively.[3] (See the article "Rubbing and Scrubbing" by Georg Hähner and Nicholas Spencer in PHYSICS TODAY, September 1998, page 22.) In general, geophysical stick-slip occurs in the following sequence: The tectonic loading stress accumulates until it exceeds the frictional stress; sliding begins; the loading stress drops below that of friction; the fault motion stops; and the process repeats. "Sticking" requires that the loading

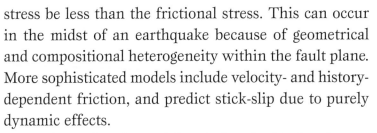

stress be less than the frictional stress. This can occur in the midst of an earthquake because of geometrical and compositional heterogeneity within the fault plane. More sophisticated models include velocity- and history-dependent friction, and predict stick-slip due to purely dynamic effects.

Both small-scale spatial variations in frictional properties and dynamic effects control the physics of seismic slip on a microscopic level. However, earthquakes are inherently large events with slip displacements as large as 10 m and particle velocities up to 3 m/s. It is important that earthquake physicists develop theoretical tools to understand how microscopic processes produce the observed macroscopic behavior.

Seismic waves radiated during earthquakes provide evidence that the properties on a fault plane are indeed complex. Seismologists can use data from modern broadband seismometers to invert observed waveforms and obtain the distribution of slip on a fault plane. Figure 3 shows the total slip on the fault plane that occurred during the 1992 Landers, California, earthquake. (See PHYSICS TODAY, September 1993, page 17.) [See original article for figure.] Such maps demonstrate that small-scale processes are inherently part of the earthquake process.

The irregular distribution of slip reflects both the complexity of dynamic frictional stress and the heterogeneity of local strength on the fault surface. Structure on finer scales than shown in the figure is likely to be present, but must be omitted from the inversion because of bandwidth limitations. The highest-frequency waves, which sample the smallest-scale structure, are filtered out because of the difficulty in modeling them. At frequencies greater than 0.5 Hz, the scattering of waves and other seismic complexities produce waveforms that cannot be explained with a simple model. Thus, models typically generate what should be regarded as low-pass filtered rupture patterns; the real slip distribution is probably far more complex with short-wavelength irregularities. Short-period seismic waves seen on seismograms and felt by people are generally believed to be caused by a fractal distribution of small fault-slip zones, each zone radiating short-period waves.

Slip distributions can be obtained at various times while earthquakes are in progress. Slip is typically heterogeneous in time, just as it is in space. By analyzing slip in both space and time, earthquake scientists can gain insight into rupture dynamics.

Rupture Dynamics and Energy

The limited resolution of seismic methods prohibits earthquake physicists from determining every detail of rupture patterns on irregular fault planes. The stress-time histories obtained through rupture patterns are therefore complemented by measurements of such integrated quantities as the total radiated energy, E_R, and the seismic moment, M_0, which gives the total amount of slip.

Ultimately one needs to consider the energy budget for an extended fault zone, but a relatively simple spring system nicely elucidates how energy is partitioned during an earthquake. The spring is initially stretched a distance, x_0, from its equilibrium length by a force, f_0.

This corresponds to the state before an earthquake. The stretched spring is held against a wall with static friction that balances f_0. During an earthquake, some energy is used to fracture rocks; this may be modeled in the spring system by attaching an arm to the spring that scratches the wall. When friction drops to the kinetic value, f_f, presumed to happen instantly for simplicity, the spring begins to recoil under a driving force, $f_0 - f_f$, scratching the wall as it goes.

Eventually the spring stops at x_1, with a displacement $d = x_0 - x_1$ when the force is f_1. Various mechanisms can stop the motion, for example geometrical or compositional heterogeneity of the wall, so that f_1 is not necessarily equal to f_f.

The frictional energy loss is $E_F = df_f$, and the total potential energy change, including strain and gravitational potential energy changes, is $\Delta W = 1/2(f_0 + f_1) d$. While the tip of the arm scratches the wall during motion, some energy, E_R, is radiated as elastic (seismic) waves, and some fracture energy, E_G, is spent mechanically damaging the surface. Conservation of energy requires $E_R = \Delta W - E_F - E_G$. The spring system just discussed is analogous to the earthquake model in box 1 and describes earthquake energetics fairly accurately if f_0, f_1, and f_f are replaced by $S\sigma_0$, $S\sigma_1$, and $S\sigma_f$, respectively, and d is replaced by D [see original article for box]. Thus, for earthquakes,

$$\Delta W = DS(\sigma_0 + \sigma_1)/2,$$
$$E_F = DS\sigma_f, \text{ and}$$
$$E_R = \Delta W - E_F - E_G.$$

As discussed in box 1, the absolute values of the stresses σ_0 and σ_1 cannot be determined. This is a serious limitation, in that seismologists cannot determine ΔW. However, since the final stress on the fault must be non-negative they can determine a lower bound for ΔW. In that case,

$$\Delta W = DS(\sigma_0 + \sigma_1)/2 \geq DS(\sigma_0 - \sigma_1)/2 = DS\Delta\sigma_s /2 \equiv \Delta W_0 .$$

Seismologists, through observations, determine $\Delta\sigma_s$, which fixes ΔW_0, the lower bound of ΔW.

Because of complex wave propagation effects, the radiated energy, E_R, has also not been measured accurately. With the advent of new instrumentation and new data from deep (about 2 km) down-hole seismographs, accurate energy estimates are becoming available, allowing earthquake physicists to study this problem more quantitatively.

A comparison of E_R and ΔW_0 measured for the 1994 deep Bolivian earthquake (M = 8.3) yields an interesting result[5] (also see PHYSICS TODAY, October 1994, page 17). This earthquake, the largest deep-focus earthquake ever recorded, occurred at a depth of 635 km. The comparison shows that $\Delta W_0 = 1.4 \times 10^{18}$ J and $E_R = 5 \times 10^{16}$ J, which is only 3 % of ΔW_0. The difference, $\Delta W_0 - E_R = 1.35 \times 10^{18}$ J, was not radiated, and must have been deposited near the focal region, probably in the form of thermal energy. That energy, about 10^{18} J, is comparable to the total thermal energy released during large volcanic eruptions such as Mount Saint Helens in 1980. Moreover, the thermal energy must have been released in a relatively small area, about $50 \times 50 \text{ km}^2$, within a time span of about 1 minute. The mechanical part of the process, the seismic waves accompanying the earthquake, was only a small component. Thus, the Bolivian earthquake was more of a thermal event than a mechanical one.

With such a large quantity of nonradiated energy, the temperature in the focal region of the Bolivian earthquake must have risen significantly. The actual temperature rise, ΔT, depends on the thickness of the fault zone, which is not known, but for a zone whose thickness is only a few centimeters, the temperature could have risen to above $5000\,°C$.

Shallow Earthquakes and Many "If"s

Although the pressure-temperature environment for shallow earthquakes may be different from that for deep earthquakes, a simple calculation shows that if σ_f is comparable to $\Delta\sigma_s$ and $\Delta\sigma_d$, about 10 MPa, then the effect of shear heating is significant. If the thermal energy is contained within a zone a few centimeters thick around the slip plane during seismic slip, the temperature can easily rise to $100–1000\,°C$. If a fault zone is dry, melting may occur and friction may drop. If some fluid exists in that zone, the thermal energy will expand the fluid, which could reduce the normal stress on points of contact between the two fault planes and thus reduce the frictional stress. The key question is how thick the fault slip zone is. Geologists have examined many exhumed faults. Some of them have a very thin (about 1-mm) distinct region where fault slips seem to have occurred repeatedly.[6] In other cases, several thin slip zones were found, but evidence shows that each represents a distinct earthquake. Thus, geological evidence suggests a thin slip zone, at least for some faults, but the question remains debatable.

The energy budget of earthquakes provides more insight into the stresses occurring in fault zones. Figure 4 shows the observed ratio, E_R/M_0, which specifies how much energy is radiated from a unit fault area per unit slip [see original article for figure]. Using the definition of M_0 given in box 1, one can write

$$E_R/M_0 = \frac{E_R}{\mu SD} = \frac{1}{\mu}\frac{(E_R/S)}{D}.$$

Although the measurement errors are still large, figure 4 indicates that the ratio for large earthquakes ($M > 5$) is 10–100 times larger than that for small events ($M < 2.5$). The increase in the ratio suggests some drastic change in fault dynamics between small and large earthquakes.[7] Box 2 on page 39 describes some possible mechanisms for such a change [see original article for box].

Earthquakes as Complex Systems

Large-magnitude earthquakes are rare events. To a very good approximation, the rate of occurrence of earthquakes falls exponentially as a function of magnitude . . . This exponential fall is called the Gutenberg-Richter relation. Several mathematical models that reproduce this relation have been proposed, including a mechanical slider-block system,[8] a percolation model,[9] and a sandpile model.[10] Here we consider a one-dimensional branching model, essentially a percolation model. We numerically model a seismic fault as a distribution of many small patches, or areas; if one patch fails, it can trigger failures in patches at s nearby sites with a transition probability p. The product $e = ps$ is the expectancy of the number of failed patches at each step.

If $e < 1$, then the growth of the failing region will eventually stop when a total of F patches has failed. The whole process corresponds to an earthquake rupture. If the simulation is repeated many times, we find a power-law-like relation between $\log F$ and the number of cases, n, in which at least F patches failed. Figure 5b shows the results of numerical simulations performed for $s = 10$ and three values of the expectancy, $e = 0.8$, 0.9, and 0.99 [see original article for figure]. As the expectancy approaches 1, the plots of figure 5b tend to linearity, corresponding to the Gutenberg-Richter relation. But also, as e approaches 1, there is occasional runaway triggering, which would indicate an exceptionally large earthquake violating the Gutenberg-Richter relation.[11] Certain mature faults, such as the San Andreas fault in California, do exhibit an anomalously large number of very-large-magnitude earthquakes. There have been more earthquakes with $M \approx 8$ on the San Andreas fault than predicted by the Gutenberg-Richter relation and relatively few earthquakes with magnitudes between 6 and 7. This deviation from the expected relation suggests a runaway process such as that found in the model. Thus, earthquake processes can exhibit the behavior of complex systems, and the percolation model—as well as the slider-block system and sand-pile model—has built-in features that mimic this behavior.

Both the shear heating and the elastohydrodynamic lubrication discussed in box 2 tend to promote slip motion as the earthquake becomes larger, that is, the slip growth rate depends nonlinearly on the slip itself [see original article for box 2]. Lubrication may thus be one of the physical mechanisms that causes earthquakes to behave as complex systems.

For long-term seismic hazard assessment, it would be useful to know how large an area of the fault is close to failure; the size of the earthquake will ultimately be determined by the size of this critical area. It would also be helpful to know just how close the critical area is to failure. Figure 5b suggests that the degree of criticality, analogous to the expectancy in the branching-model simulation, could, in principle, be diagnosed by measuring the slope of the magnitude-frequency relationship for the area. (In this context, "frequency" refers to the occurrence rate of earthquakes.) Although it may be difficult to determine the degree of criticality with seismic data alone, the concept of criticality is important because it suggests the use of other methods to monitor the state of the crust. For example, electromagnetic methods could be used to monitor fluid flow in the crust. When fluid migrates in the crust and weakens some parts of fault zones, the crust could approach a critical state and produce electrical or magnetic noise. If the crust has a low degree of criticality, a small perturbation in stress or weakness is not very likely to cause a large event.

Connecting Small and Large Scales

A number of approaches link observations with mechanics in earthquake physics. The fundamental problem is to understand the microscopic processes using macroscopically observed parameters. We who study earthquakes, like those who established statistical mechanics, must develop methods to connect radically different size scales.

One microscopic feature is of particular interest to us: the thin fault zone. During large seismic events, thermal and mechanical processes may result in low friction in such zones. This low friction, combined with estimated static and dynamic stress drops, suggests that mature seismic fault systems operate at relatively low stresses, on the order of tens of MPa. On the other hand, the crust supports large surface loads, such as mountains, that require its strength to be at least 100 MPa. This means that the stress in the crust is spatially extremely heterogeneous, and the system organizes itself into a somewhat precarious state with low stress on major faults.

But what happens during an earthquake? In the self-organized system just described, a small stress perturbation can trigger a seismic event. The growth of the earthquake is controlled by heterogeneous friction on the fault, which in turn may be affected by nonlinear processes involved in lubricated dynamic slip. This growth process results in the standard magnitude-frequency relationship with occasional unusually large earthquakes, possibly caused by large runaway events. Elastohydrodynamic lubrication in a thin fault zone may change the roughness of the fault plane and thereby change the frequency spectrum of ground motion. Strategies for designing structures that will withstand ground motions from large earthquakes would have to account for this change in frequency spectrum. The lubrication model we have proposed is new, and debate continues about the microscopic processes occurring in the fault zone. Understanding these processes is key to a better understanding of seismicity, rupture dynamics, and ground motion characteristics, which will lead to effective seismic risk mitigation measures.

References

1. Some good general references are: K. Aki, P. G. Richards, *Quantitative Seismology*, Freeman, San Francisco (1980); B. A. Bolt, *Earthquakes*, Freeman, New York (1999); T. Lay, T. C. Wallace, *Modern Global Seismology*, Academic Press, New York (1995); C. H. Scholz, *The Mechanics of Earthquakes and Faulting*, Cambridge U. Press, New York (1990).
2. C. Tsuboi, Bull. *Earthquake Res. Inst., U. Tokyo* **10**, 411 (1932).
3. E. Rabinowicz, *Friction and Wear of Materials*, Wiley, New York (1995).
4. D. J. Wald, T. H. Heaton, *Bull. Seismol. Soc. Am.* **84**, 668 (1994).
5. H. Kanamori, T. H. Anderson, T. H. Heaton, *Science* **279**, 839 (1998).
6. F. M. Chester, J. S. Chester, *Tectonophysics* **295**, 199 (1998).
7. H. Kanamori, T. Heaton, in *GeoComplexity and the Physics of Earthquakes*, J. R. Rundle, D. L. Turcotte, W. Klein, eds., Geophysical monograph no. 120, American Geophysical Union, Washington, DC (2000), p. 147.
8. R. Burridge, L. Knopoff, *Bull. Seismol. Soc. Am.* **57**, 341 (1967).
9. M. Otsuka, *Zisin* **24**, 215 (1971).
10. P. Bak, C. Tang, *J. Geophys. Res.* **94**, 15 635 (1989).
11. H. Kanamori, J. Mori, in *Problems in Geophysics for the New Millennium: A Collection of Papers in Honor of Adam M. Dziewonski*, E. Bochi, G. Ekström, A. Morelli eds., Compositori, Bologna, Italy (2000), p. 73. See, in particular, fig. 9.
12. E. E. Brodsky, H. Kanamori, *J. Geophys. Res.* (in press).
13. K-F. Ma, C-T. Lee, Y-B. Tsai, T. C. Shin, J. Mori, *EOS Transactions* **80**, 605 (1999).
14. R. Abercrombie, *J. Geophys. Res.* **100**, 24.

On December 26, 2004, an earthquake measuring 9.0 on the Richter scale struck off the coast of Sumatra, an Indonesian island. This massive release of seismic energy created a disturbance in the Indian Ocean that gave rise to a devastating tsunami, a deadly series of powerful waves. Like the concentric ripples created after a stone is dropped in water, the tsunami radiated outward hundreds of miles to strike in successive waves the coasts of Indonesia, Malaysia, Thailand, Myanmar, Bangladesh, India, Sri Lanka, Madagascar, Somalia, Kenya, Tanzania, and South Africa. It seems likely that well over 300,000 people were killed in the resulting flooding, and entire villages were destroyed and swept out to sea.

How is a tsunami formed, and what accounts for its astonishing power? Most tsunamis form as a result of earthquakes beneath the ocean or in coastal areas. Less frequently, they can result from landslides, volcanic eruptions, and even meteorite strikes. The large amount of water displaced by an earthquake or other major disturbance forms waves as the displaced water seeks equilibrium again. These waves are known as shallow-water waves. Normal wind-generated waves are generally spaced at five to twenty second intervals. This is known as the waves' period. They can be about 300 to 600 feet (100 to 200 meters) apart (their wavelength). Shallow-water waves, like tsunamis, can have a *period of 10 to 120 minutes and a wavelength of 300 miles (500 kilometers). The larger a wave's wavelength, the less energy it loses as it moves toward land and the faster it travels. Some tsunamis have been known to travel more than 500 miles per hour (800 kilometers per hour), the same speed as a commercial jet. The December 2004 tsunami was traveling at about 300 mph (480 km/hr). As the tsunami approaches the shallow water near coastlines, it begins to slow, but its energy remains the same, increasing the height of the wave. While tsunamis are hardly visible in the open ocean, as they approach land their height can increase from a couple of feet (0.61 m) to as much as 100 feet (30 m). The result can be the massive flooding and widespread destruction seen in December 2004.*

In this article, Frank I. González takes a closer look at the generation, motion, and destructive force of tsunamis from a physics-based perspective, a perspective that may one day help save lives by providing tsunami predictions and early warnings for coastal communities. —LEH

"Tsunami!"
by Frank I. González
Scientific American, May 1999

The sun had set 12 minutes earlier, and twilight was waning on the northern coast of Papua New Guinea. It was July 17, 1998, and another tranquil Friday evening was drawing to a close for the men, women and children of Sissano, Arop, Warapu and other small villages on the peaceful sand spit between Sissano Lagoon and the Bismarck Sea. But deep in the earth, far beneath the wooden huts of the unsuspecting villagers, tremendous forces had strained the underlying rock for years. Now, in the space of minutes, this pent-up energy violently released as a magnitude 7.1 earthquake. At 6:49 p.m., the main shock rocked 30 kilometers (nearly 19 miles) of coastline centered on the lagoon and suddenly deformed the offshore ocean bottom. The normally flat sea surface lurched upward in response, giving birth to a fearsome tsunami.

Retired Colonel John Sanawe, who lived near the southeast end of the sandbar at Arop, survived the tsunami and later told his story to Hugh Davies of the University of Papua New Guinea. Just after the main shock struck only 20 kilometers offshore, Sanawe saw the sea rise above the horizon and then spray vertically perhaps 30 meters. Unexpected sounds—first like distant thunder, then like a nearby helicopter—gradually faded as he watched the sea slowly recede below the normal low-water mark. After four or five minutes of silence, he heard a rumble like that of a low-flying jet plane. Sanawe spotted the first tsunami wave, perhaps three or four meters high. He tried to run home, but the wave overtook him. A second, larger wave flattened the village and swept him a kilometer into a mangrove forest on the inland shore of the lagoon.

Other villagers were not so fortunate as Sanawe. Some were swept across the lagoon and impaled on the broken mangrove branches. Many more were viciously battered by debris. At least 30 survivors would lose injured limbs to gangrene. Saltwater crocodiles and wild dogs preyed on the dead before help could arrive, making it more difficult to arrive at an exact death toll. It now appears that the tsunami killed more than 2,200 villagers, including more than 230 children. Waves up to 15 meters high, which struck within 15 minutes of the main shock, had caught many coastal inhabitants unawares. Of the few villagers who knew of the tsunami hazard, those trapped on the sandbar simply had no safe place to flee.

Tsunamis such as those that pounded Papua New Guinea are the world's most powerful waves. Historical patterns of their occurrence are revealed in large databases developed by James F. Lander, Patricia A. Lockridge and their colleagues at the National Geophysical Data Center in Boulder, Colo., and Viacheslav K. Gusiakov and his associates at the Tsunami Laboratory in Novosibirsk, Russia. Most tsunamis afflict the Pacific Ocean, and 86 percent of those are the products of undersea earthquakes around the Pacific Rim, where powerful collisions of tectonic plates form highly seismic subduction zones.

Since 1990, 10 tsunamis have taken more than 4,000 lives. In all, 82 were reported worldwide—a rate much higher than the historical average of 57 a decade. The increase in tsunamis reported is due to improved global communications; the high death tolls are partly due to increases in coastal populations. My colleagues and I at the National Oceanic and Atmospheric Administration Pacific Marine Environmental Laboratory in Seattle set up an electronic-mail network as a way for researchers in distant parts of the world to help one another make faster and more accurate tsunami surveys. This Tsunami Bulletin Board, now managed by the International Tsunami Information Center, has facilitated communication among tsunami scientists since shortly after the 1992 Nicaragua tsunami.

Disasters similar to those in Nicaragua and Papua New Guinea have wreaked havoc in Hawaii and Alaska in the past, but most tsunami researchers had long believed that the U.S. West Coast was relatively safe from the most devastating events. New evidence now suggests that earthquakes may give birth to large tsunamis every 300 to 700 years along the Cascadia subduction zone, an area off the Pacific Northwest coast where a crustal plate carrying part of the Pacific Ocean is diving under North America. A clear reminder of this particular threat occurred in April 1992, when a magnitude 7.1 earthquake at the southern end of the subduction zone generated a small tsunami near Cape Mendocino, Calif. This event served as the wake-up call that has driven the development of the first systematic national effort to prepare for dangerous tsunamis before they strike. The Pacific Marine Environmental Laboratory is playing a key research and management role in this endeavor.

The Physics of Tsunamis

To understand tsunamis, it is first helpful to distinguish them from wind-generated waves or tides. Breezes blowing across the ocean crinkle the surface into relatively short waves that create currents restricted to a shallow layer; a scuba diver, for example, might easily swim deep enough to find calm water. Strong gales are able to whip up waves 30 meters or higher in the open ocean, but even these do not move deep water.

Tides, which sweep around the globe twice a day, do produce currents that reach the ocean bottom— just as tsunamis do. Unlike true tidal waves, however, tsunamis are not generated by the gravitational pull of the moon or sun. A tsunami is produced impulsively by an undersea earthquake or, much less frequently, by volcanic eruptions, meteorite impacts or underwater landslides. With speeds that can exceed 700 kilometers per hour in the deep ocean, a tsunami wave could easily keep pace with a Boeing 747. Despite its high speed, a tsunami is not dangerous in deep water. A single wave is less than a few meters high, and its length can extend more than 750 kilometers in the open ocean. This creates a sea-surface slope so gentle that the wave usually passes unnoticed in deep water. In fact, the Japanese word tsu-nami translates literally as "harbor wave," perhaps because a tsunami can speed silently and undetected across the ocean, then unexpectedly arise as destructively high waves in shallow coastal waters.

A powerful tsunami also has a very long reach: it can transport destructive energy from its source to coastlines thousands of kilometers away. Hawaii, because of its midocean location, is especially vulnerable to such Pacific-wide tsunamis. Twelve damaging tsunamis have struck Hawaii since 1895. In the most destructive, 159 people died there in 1946 from killer waves generated almost 3,700 kilometers away in Alaska's Aleutian

Islands. Such remote-source tsunamis can strike unexpectedly, but local-source tsunamis—as in the case of last year's Papua New Guinea disaster—can be especially devastating. Lander has estimated that more than 90 percent of all fatalities occur within about 200 kilometers of the source. As an extreme example, it is believed that a tsunami killed more than 30,000 people within 120 kilometers of the catastrophic eruption of Krakatoa volcano in the Sunda Straits of Indonesia in 1883. That explosion generated waves as high as a 12-story building.

Regardless of their origin, tsunamis evolve through three overlapping but quite distinct physical processes: generation by any force that disturbs the water column, propagation from deeper water near the source to shallow coastal areas and, finally, inundation of dry land. Of these, the propagation phase is best understood, whereas generation and inundation are more difficult to model with computer simulations. Accurate simulations are important in predicting where future remote-source tsunamis will strike and in guiding disaster surveys and rescue efforts, which must concentrate their resources on regions believed to be hardest hit.

Generation is the process by which a seafloor disturbance, such as movement along a fault, reshapes the sea surface into a tsunami. Modelers assume that this sea-surface displacement is identical to that of the ocean bottom, but direct measurements of seafloor motion have never been available (and may never be). Instead researchers use an idealized model of the quake: they assume that the crustal plates slip past one another along a simple, rectangular plane inside the earth. Even then, predicting the tsunami's initial height requires at least 10 descriptive parameters, including the amount of slip on each side of the imaginary plane and its length and width. As modelers scramble to guide tsunami survey teams immediately after an earthquake, only the orientation of the assumed fault plane and the quake's location, magnitude and depth can be interpreted from the seismic data alone. All other parameters must be estimated. As a consequence, this first simulation frequently underestimates inundation, sometimes by factors of 5 or 10.

Low inundation estimates can signify that the initial tsunami height was also understated because the single-plane fault model distributes seismic energy over too large an area. Analyses of seismic data cannot resolve energy distribution patterns any shorter than the seismic waves themselves, which extend for several hundred kilometers. But long after the tsunami strikes land, modelers can work backward from records of run-up and additional earthquake data to refine the tsunami's initial height. For example, months of aftershocks eventually reveal patterns of seismic energy that are concentrated in regions much smaller than the original, single-plane fault model assumed. When seismic energy is focused in a smaller area, the vertical motion of the seafloor—and therefore the initial tsunami height—is greater. Satisfactory simulations are achieved only after months of labor-intensive work, but every simulation that matches the real disaster improves scientists' ability to make better predictions.

Propagation of the tsunami transports seismic energy away from the earthquake site through undulations of the water, just as shaking moves the energy through the earth. At this point, the wave height is so small compared with both the wavelength and the water depth that researchers apply linear wave theory, which assumes that the height itself does not affect the wave's behavior. The theory predicts that the deeper the water and the longer the wave, the faster the tsunami. This dependence of wave speed on water depth means that refraction by bumps and grooves on the seafloor can shift the wave's direction, especially as it travels into shallow water. In particular, wave fronts tend to align parallel to the shoreline so that they wrap around a protruding headland before smashing into it with greatly focused incident energy. At the same time, each individual wave must also slow down because of the decreasing water depth, so they begin to overtake one another, decreasing the distance between them in a process called shoaling. Refraction and shoaling squeeze the same amount of energy into a smaller volume of water, creating higher waves and faster currents.

The last stage of evolution, inundation and run-up, in which a tsunami may run ashore as a breaking wave, a wall of water or a tidelike flood, is perhaps the most difficult to model. The wave height is now so large that linear theory fails to describe the complicated interaction between the water and the shoreline. Vertical run-up can reach tens of meters, but it typically takes only two to three meters to cause damage. Horizontal inundation, if unimpeded by coastal cliffs or other steep topography, can penetrate hundreds of meters inland. Both kinds of flooding are aided and abetted by the typical crustal displacement of a subduction zone earthquake, which lifts the offshore ocean bottom and lowers the land along the coast. This type of displacement propagates waves seaward with a leading crest and landward with a leading trough (the reason a receding sea sometimes precedes a tsunami). Not only does the near-shore subsidence facilitate tsunami penetration inland but, according to recent studies by Raissa Mazova of the Nizhny Novgorod State Technical University in Russia and by Costas Synolakis of the University of Southern California, both theoretical predictions and field surveys indicate that coastal run-up and inundation will be greater if the trough of the leading wave precedes the crest.

Preparation and Warnings Save Lives

Predicting where a tsunami may strike helps to save lives and property only if coastal inhabitants recognize the threat and respond appropriately. More than a quarter of all reliably reported Pacific tsunamis since 1895 originated near Japan. This is not surprising, because Japan is precariously situated near the colliding margins of four tectonic plates. Recognizing the recurring threat, the Japanese have invested heavily over the years in tsunami hazard mitigation, including comprehensive educational and public outreach programs, an effective warning system, shoreline barrier forests, seawalls and other coastal fortifications.

On the night of July 12, 1993, their preparations faced a brutal test. A magnitude 7.8 earthquake in the

Sea of Japan generated a tsunami that struck various parts of the small island of Okushiri. Five minutes after the main shock the Japan Meteorological Agency issued a warning over television and radio that a major tsunami was on its way. By then, 10- to 20-meter waves had struck the coastline nearest the source, claiming a number of victims before they could flee. In Aonae, a small fishing village on the island's southern peninsula, many of the 1,600 townspeople fled to high ground as soon as they felt the main shock. A few minutes later tsunami waves five to 10 meters high ravaged hundreds of their homes and businesses and swept them out to sea. More than 200 lives were lost in this disaster, but quick response saved many more.

Over the past century in Japan, approximately 15 percent of 150 tsunamis were damaging or fatal. That track record is much better than the tally in countries with few or no community education programs in place. For example, more than half of the 34 tsunamis that struck Indonesia in the past 100 years were damaging or fatal. Interviews conducted after the 1992 Flores Island tsunami that killed more than 1,000 people indicated that most coastal residents did not recognize the earthquake as the natural warning of a possible tsunami and did not flee inland. Similarly, Papua New Guinea residents were tragically uninformed, sending the number of casualties from last year's disaster higher than expected for a tsunami of that size. A large quake in 1907 evidently lowered the area that is now Sissano Lagoon, but any resulting tsunami was too small and too long ago to imprint a community memory. When the earthquake struck last year, some people actually walked to the coast to investigate the disturbance, thus sealing their fate.

Scientists have learned a great deal from recent tsunamis, but centuries-old waves continue to yield valuable insights. Lander and his colleagues have described more than 200 tsunamis known to have affected the U.S. since the time of the first written records in Alaska and the Caribbean during the early 1700s and in Hawaii and along the West Coast later that century. Total damage is estimated at half a billion dollars and 470 casualties, primarily in Alaska and Hawaii. An immediate threat to those states and the West Coast is the Alaska-Aleutian subduction zone. Included in this region's history of large, tsunami-generating earthquakes are two disasters that drove the establishment of the country's only two tsunami warning centers. The probability of a magnitude 7.4 or greater earthquake occurring somewhere in this zone before 2008 is estimated to be 84 percent.

Another major threat, unrevealed by the written records, lurks off the coasts of Washington State, Oregon and northern California—the Cascadia subduction zone. Brian F. Atwater of the U.S. Geological Survey has identified sand and gravel deposits that he hypothesized were carried inland from the Washington coast by tsunamis born of Cascadia quakes. Recent events support this theory. The Nicaragua tsunami was notable for the amount of sand it transported inland, and researchers have documented similar deposits at inundation sites in Flores, Okushiri, Papua New Guinea and elsewhere.

At least one segment of the Cascadia subduction zone may be approaching the end of a seismic cycle that culminates in an earthquake and destructive tsunami [see "Giant Earthquakes of the Pacific Northwest," by Roy D. Hyndman; *Scientific American*, December 1995]. The earthquake danger is believed to be comparable to that in southern California—about a 35 percent probability of occurrence before 2045. Finally, the 1992 Cape Mendocino earthquake and tsunami was a clear reminder that the Cascadia subduction zone can unleash local tsunamis that strike the coast within minutes.

Getting Ready in the U.S.

Hard on the heels of the surprising Cape Mendocino tsunami, the Federal Emergency Management Agency (FEMA) and NOAA funded an earthquake scenario study of northern California and the production of tsunami inundation maps for Eureka and Crescent City in that state. The resulting "all hazards" map was the first of its kind for the U.S. It delineates areas susceptible to tsunami flooding, earthquake-shaking intensity, liquefaction and landslides. Researchers then tackled the possible effects of a great Cascadia subduction zone earthquake and tsunami. About 300,000 people live or work in nearby coastal regions, and at least as many tourists travel through these areas every year. Local tsunami waves could strike communities within minutes of a big quake, leaving little or no time to issue formal warnings. What is more, a Cascadia-born tsunami disaster could cost the region between $1.25 billion and $6.25 billion, a conservative estimate considering the 1993 Okushiri disaster.

Clarification of the threat from the Cascadia subduction zone and the many well-reported tsunami disasters of this decade have stimulated a systematic effort to examine the tsunami hazard in the U.S. In 1997 Congress provided $2.3 million to establish the National Tsunami Hazard Mitigation Program. Alaska, California, Hawaii, Oregon and Washington formed a partnership with NOAA, FEMA and the USGS to tackle the threat of both local- and remote-source tsunamis. The partnership focuses on three interlocking activities: assessing the threat to specific coastal areas; improving early detection of tsunamis and their potential danger; and educating communities to ensure an appropriate response when a tsunami strikes.

The threat to specific coastal areas can be assessed by means of tsunami inundation maps such as those designed for Eureka and Crescent City using state-of-the-art computer modeling. These maps provide critical guidance to local emergency planners charged with identifying evacuation routes. Only Hawaii has systematically developed such maps over the years. To date, three Oregon communities have received maps, six additional maps are in progress in Oregon, Washington and California, and three maps are planned for Alaska.

Rapid, reliable confirmation of the existence of a potentially dangerous tsunami is essential to officials responsible for sounding alarms. Coastal tide gauges have been specially modified to measure tsunamis, and a major upgrade of the seismic network will soon provide more rapid and more complete reports on the nature of the earthquake. These instruments are essential to the warning system, but seismometers measure earthquakes, not tsunamis. And although tide gauges spot tsunamis close to shore, they cannot measure tsunami energy propagating toward a distant coastline. As a consequence, an unacceptable 75 percent false-alarm rate has prevailed since the 1950s. These incidents are expensive, undermine the credibility of the warning system, and place citizens at risk during the evacuation. A false alarm that triggered the evacuation of Honolulu on May 7, 1986, cost Hawaii more than $30 million in lost salaries and business revenues

NOAA is therefore developing a network of six deep-ocean reporting stations that can track tsunamis and report them in real time, a project known as Deep-Ocean Assessment and Reporting of Tsunamis (DART). Scientists have completed testing of prototype systems and expect the network to be operating reliably in two years. The rationale for this type of warning system is simple: if an earthquake strikes off the coast of Alaska while you're lying on a Hawaiian beach, what you really want to have between you and the quake's epicenter is a DART system. Here's why:

Seismometers staked out around the Pacific Rim can almost instantly pinpoint a big Alaskan quake's location. In the next moment, complex computer programs can predict how long a triggered tsunami would take to reach Hawaii, even though there is not yet evidence a wave exists. After some minutes, tide gauges scattered along the coastlines may detect a tsunami. But the only way to be sure whether a dangerous wave is headed toward a distant coast is to place tsunami detectors in its path and track it across the open ocean.

Conceptually, the idea of such a real-time reporting network is straightforward; however, formidable technological and logistical challenges have held up implementation until now. The DART systems depend on bottom pressure recorders that Hugh B. Milburn, Alex Nakamura, Eddie N. Bernard and I have been perfecting over the past decade at the Pacific Marine Environmental Laboratory. As the crest of a tsunami wave passes by, the bottom recorder detects the increased pressure from the additional volume of overlying water. Even 6,000 meters deep, the sensitive instrument can detect a tsunami no higher than a single centimeter. Ship and storm waves are not detected, because their length is short and, as with currents, changes in pressure are not transmitted all the way to the ocean bottom. We placed the first recorders on the north Pacific seafloor in 1986 and have been using them to record tsunamis ever since. The records cannot be accessed, however, until the instruments are retrieved.

Ideally, when the bottom recorders detect a tsunami, acoustic chirps will transmit the measurements to a car-size buoy at the ocean surface, which will then relay the information to a ground station via satellite. The surface buoy systems, the satellite relay technology and the bottom recorders have proved themselves at numerous deep-ocean stations, including an array of 70 weather buoys set up along the equator to track El Niño, the oceanographic phenomenon so infamous for its effect on world climate. The biggest challenge has been developing a reliable acoustic transmission system. Over the past three years, four prototype DART systems have been deployed, worked for a time, then failed. Design improvements to a second-generation system have refined communication between the bottom recorders and the buoys.

In the next two years, our laboratory plans to establish five stations spread across the north Pacific from the west Aleutians to Oregon and a sixth sited on the equator to intercept tsunamis generated off South America. More buoys would reduce the possibility that tsunami waves might sneak between them, but the current budget limits the number that NOAA can afford. This is where detailed computer simulations become invaluable. Combined with the buoy measurements, the simulations will provide more accurate predictions to guide officials who may have only a few minutes to decide whether to sound an alarm.

Even the most reliable warning is ineffective if people do not respond appropriately. Community education is thus perhaps the most important aspect of the national mitigation program's threefold mission. Each state is identifying coordinators who will provide information and guidance to community emergency managers during tsunami disasters. Interstate coordination is also crucial to public safety because U.S. citizens are highly mobile, and procedures must be compatible from state to state. Standard tsunami signage has already been put in place along many coastlines.

Tsunami researchers and emergency response officials agree that future destructive tsunamis are inevitable and technology alone cannot save lives. Coastal inhabitants must be able to recognize the signs of a possible tsunami—such as strong, prolonged ground shaking—and know that they should seek higher ground immediately. Coastal communities need inundation maps that identify far in advance what areas are likely to be flooded so that they can lay out evacuation routes. The proactive enterprise now under way in the U.S. will surely upgrade tsunami prediction for a much larger region of the Pacific. All of these efforts are essential to the overriding goal of avoiding tragedies such as those in Papua New Guinea, Nicaragua and elsewhere.

Reprinted with permission from Frank I. Gonzalez.

Web Sites

Due to the changing nature of Internet links, the Rosen Publishing Group, Inc., has developed an online list of Web sites related to the subject of this book. This site is updated regularly. Please use this link to access the list:

http://www.rosenlinks.com/cdfp/lamo

For Further Reading

Baierlein, Ralph. *Newtonian Dynamics*. New York, NY: McGraw-Hill Science/Engineering/Math, 1983.

Dalitz, Richard H., and Michael Navenberg, eds. *The Foundations of Newtonian Scholarship*. Hackensack, NJ: World Scientific Publishing Co., 2000.

Feingold, Mordechai. *The Newtonian Moment: Isaac Newton and the Making of Modern Culture*. New York, NY: Oxford University Press, 2004.

Gibilisco, Stan. *Physics Demystified: A Self-Teaching Guide*. New York, NY: McGraw-Hill Professional, 2002.

Krane, Kenneth S. *Modern Physics*. New York, NY: Wiley, 1995.

Lange, Marc. *An Introduction to the Philosophy of Physics: Locality, Fields, Energy, and Mass*. Malden, MA: Blackwell Publishers, 2002.

Lightman, Alan P. *Great Ideas in Physics*. New York, NY: McGraw-Hill, 2000.

Rothman, Tony. *Instant Physics: From Aristotle to Einstein, and Beyond*. New York, NY: Ballantine Books, 1995.

Bibliography

Asai, Takeshi, and Takao Akatsuka. "The Physics of
    Football." PhysicsWeb. June 1998. Retrieved
    September 2004 (http://physicsweb.org/
    articles/world/11/6/8/1#world-11-6-8-1).
Astumian, R. Dean, and Peter Hänggi. "Brownian
    Motors." *Physics Today*, November 2002,
    pp. 33–39.
Baugh, Richard A. "Dynamics of Spear Throwing."
    American Journal of Physics, Vol. 71, No. 4,
    April 2003.
Bocquet, Lydéric. "The Physics of Stone Skipping."
    American Journal of Physics, Vol. 71, No. 2,
    February 2003.
Canup, Robin M. "Origin of Terrestrial Planets and
    the Earth–Moon System." *Physics Today*, April
    2004, pp. 56–62.
Cho, Adrian. "Momentum from Nothing." *Physical
    Review Focus*, January 23, 2004. Retrieved October
    2004 (http://focus.aps.org/story/v13/st3).
Crease, Robert P. "The Legend of the Leaning
    Tower." *Physics World*, February 2003. Retrieved
    October 2004 (http://physicsweb.org/articles/
    world/16/2/2/1).

Dickinson, Michael. "Animal Locomotion: How to Walk on Water." *Nature*, Vol. 424, No. 6949, August 7, 2003, pp. 621–622.

González, Frank I. "Tsunami!" *Scientific American*, Vol. 21, No. 12, May 1999, pp. 56–65.

Heller, Eric J. "Quantum Physics: Air Juggling and Other Tricks." *Nature*, Vol. 412, No. 6842, July 5, 2001, pp. 33–34.

Kanamori, Hiroo, and Emily E. Brodsky. "The Physics of Earthquakes." *Physics Today*, June 2001, pp. 34–40.

Kessler, David A. "Surface Physics: A New Crack at Friction." *Nature*, Vol. 413, No. 6853, September 20, 2001, pp. 260–261.

Krieger, Kim. "Craters in a Sandbox." *Physical Review Focus*, September 12, 2003. Retrieved October 2004 (http://focus.aps.org/story/v12/st8).

Lindley, David. "Slip-Slidin' Away." *Physical Review Focus*, June 11, 2003. Retrieved October 2004 (http://focus.aps.org/story/v11/st26).

Mackenzie, Dana. "Moon-Forming Crash Is Likely in New Model." *Science*, Vol. 283, No. 5398, January 1, 1999, pp. 15–16.

Minetti, Alberto E. "Biomechanics: Walking on Other Planets." *Nature*, Vol. 409, No. 6819, January 25, 2001, pp. 467–469.

Müller, Ulrike K., and Sander Kranenbarg. "Power at the Tip of the Tongue." *Science*, Vol. 304, No. 5668, April 9, 2004, pp. 217–219.

Pennisi, Elizabeth. "Uphill Dash May Have Led to Flight." *Science*, Vol. 299, No. 5605, January 17, 2003, p. 329.

Stewart, Ian. "Nonlinear Dynamics: Quantizing the Classical Cat." *Nature*, Vol. 430, No. 7001, August 12, 2004, pp. 731–732.

Wald, Chelsea. "Getting an Extra Bounce." *Physical Review Focus*, October 4, 2004. Retrieved October 2004 (http://focus.aps.org/story/v14/st14).

Index

About the Editor

Linley Erin Hall is a freelance writer and editor based in Berkeley, CA. Her specialty is writing about chemistry, biochemistry, and engineering, but she has also written about nanoelectronics, fluid dynamics, sleep apnea, lizard evolution, and even a four-year-old golf prodigy. Hall has a graduate certificate in science communication from the University of California, Santa Cruz, and a bachelor's degree in chemistry with emphasis on bio-chemistry from Harvey Mudd College.

Photo Credits

Front cover (clockwise from top right): "Infinite Textures" © Comstock Images Royalty-Free Division; "Bouncing Ball" © Photo Researchers, Inc.; "Liquid Crystal" © Getty Images; background image of gyroscope © Getty Images; portrait, Isaac Newton © Library of Congress, Prints and Photographs Division. Back cover: top image "Electrons Orbiting Nucleus" © Royalty-Free/Corbis; bottom "Liquid Crystal" © Getty Images.

Designer: Geri Fletcher